C-4961   CAREER EXAMINATION SERIES

This is your
PASSBOOK for...

Project Manager III/IV

Test Preparation Study Guide
Questions & Answers

COPYRIGHT NOTICE

This book is SOLELY intended for, is sold ONLY to, and its use is RESTRICTED to individual, bona fide applicants or candidates who qualify by virtue of having seriously filed applications for appropriate license, certificate, professional and/or promotional advancement, higher school matriculation, scholarship, or other legitimate requirements of education and/or governmental authorities.

This book is NOT intended for use, class instruction, tutoring, training, duplication, copying, reprinting, excerption, or adaptation, etc., by:

1) Other publishers
2) Proprietors and/or Instructors of "Coaching" and/or Preparatory Courses
3) Personnel and/or Training Divisions of commercial, industrial, and governmental organizations
4) Schools, colleges, or universities and/or their departments and staffs, including teachers and other personnel
5) Testing Agencies or Bureaus
6) Study groups which seek by the purchase of a single volume to copy and/or duplicate and/or adapt this material for use by the group as a whole without having purchased individual volumes for each of the members of the group
7) Et al.

Such persons would be in violation of appropriate Federal and State statutes.

PROVISION OF LICENSING AGREEMENTS – Recognized educational, commercial, industrial, and governmental institutions and organizations, and others legitimately engaged in educational pursuits, including training, testing, and measurement activities, may address request for a licensing agreement to the copyright owners, who will determine whether, and under what conditions, including fees and charges, the materials in this book may be used them. In other words, a licensing facility exists for the legitimate use of the material in this book on other than an individual basis. However, it is asseverated and affirmed here that the material in this book CANNOT be used without the receipt of the express permission of such a licensing agreement from the Publishers. Inquiries re licensing should be addressed to the company, attention rights and permissions department.

All rights reserved, including the right of reproduction in whole or in part, in any form or by any means, electronic or mechanical, including photocopying, recording, or by any information storage and retrieval system, without permission in writing from the Publisher.

Copyright © 2025 by
National Learning Corporation

212 Michael Drive, Syosset, NY 11791
(516) 921-8888 • www.passbooks.com
E-mail: info@passbooks.com

PASSBOOK® SERIES

THE *PASSBOOK® SERIES* has been created to prepare applicants and candidates for the ultimate academic battlefield – the examination room.

At some time in our lives, each and every one of us may be required to take an examination – for validation, matriculation, admission, qualification, registration, certification, or licensure.

Based on the assumption that every applicant or candidate has met the basic formal educational standards, has taken the required number of courses, and read the necessary texts, the *PASSBOOK® SERIES* furnishes the one special preparation which may assure passing with confidence, instead of failing with insecurity. Examination questions – together with answers – are furnished as the basic vehicle for study so that the mysteries of the examination and its compounding difficulties may be eliminated or diminished by a sure method.

This book is meant to help you pass your examination provided that you qualify and are serious in your objective.

The entire field is reviewed through the huge store of content information which is succinctly presented through a provocative and challenging approach – the question-and-answer method.

A climate of success is established by furnishing the correct answers at the end of each test.

You soon learn to recognize types of questions, forms of questions, and patterns of questioning. You may even begin to anticipate expected outcomes.

You perceive that many questions are repeated or adapted so that you can gain acute insights, which may enable you to score many sure points.

You learn how to confront new questions, or types of questions, and to attack them confidently and work out the correct answers.

You note objectives and emphases, and recognize pitfalls and dangers, so that you may make positive educational adjustments.

Moreover, you are kept fully informed in relation to new concepts, methods, practices, and directions in the field.

You discover that you are actually taking the examination all the time: you are preparing for the examination by "taking" an examination, not by reading extraneous and/or supererogatory textbooks.

In short, this PASSBOOK®, used directedly, should be an important factor in helping you to pass your test.

PROJECT MANAGER III, IV

DUTIES
Project Managers apply a wide range of specialized knowledge, skills, tools, and techniques to direct and coordinate human and material resources at all phases of a project-origination, initiation, planning, execution and control, and closeout. A project is a temporary effort with defined objectives and results undertaken to develop, modify, or enhance a product, service or system; it has a specific beginning and end date. Project Managers balance competing demands and mitigate risks to ensure the delivery of an acceptable product to stakeholders and the project sponsor that is within budget, scope, time and quality standards.

Project Managers may be assigned to a Project Management Officer or to a program area that has a continuing need for project management skills. In either assignment, the depth and breadth of skills and knowledge, and the duties performed, are comparable. Project Mangers perform tasks across all nine project management knowledge areas - project integration, scope, time, cost, quality, human resources, communications, procurement and risk. Each knowledge area includes a grouping of skills and abilities, all of which are necessary to successfully guide various activities of a project. A Project Manager must understand, identify and apply project management tools and techniques appropriate to each project phase and across the nine knowledge areas.

Project Managers III and Project Managers IV are distinguished by the depth and breadth of the knowledge areas that they must apply to successfully manage a project or portfolio of projects. The complexity of a project is determined by project scope, risk exposure, span of control, diversity of skill-sets and capabilities, and other factors such as the size of the project's budget, number of team members, and their skill level.

SCOPE OF THE EXAMINATION
The written test will cover knowledge, skills and/or abilities in such areas as:

1. **Understanding and applying administrative principles** - These questions test for knowledge of how to effectively manage and direct an organization or an organizational segment. These questions cover such areas as developing objectives, formulating policies, making decisions, forecasting and planning, developing personnel, organizing and coordinating work, communicating information, providing leadership, and delegating authority and responsibility.
2. **Preparing reports and official documents** - These questions test for the ability to prepare reports and other official documents for use within and among governmental agencies, in legal or regulatory settings, or for dissemination to the public. Some questions test for a knowledge of correct grammar, usage, punctuation, and sentence structure. Others test for the ability to use the proper tone and to express information clearly and accurately.

3. **Working and interacting with others -** These questions test for knowledge of how to effectively approach work and maintain professional relationships with others in the workplace. Each question presents a situation and a number of possible approaches for handling it. Question topics may include working with supervisors and coworkers, interacting with members of the public, handling conflict, and managing workplace demands and priorities. The questions are not specific to any job title or place of work.
4. **Supervision** These questions test for knowledge of the principles and practices employed in planning, organizing, and controlling the activities of a work unit toward predetermined objectives. The concepts covered, usually in a situational question format, include such topics as assigning and reviewing work; evaluating performance; maintaining work standards; motivating and developing subordinates; implementing procedural change; increasing efficiency; and dealing with problems of absenteeism, morale, and discipline.
5. **Administrative supervision -** These questions test for knowledge of the principles and practices involved in directing the activities of a large subordinate staff, including subordinate supervisors. Questions relate to the personal interactions between an upper level supervisor and his/her subordinate supervisors in the accomplishment of objectives. These questions cover such areas as assigning work to and coordinating the activities of several units, establishing and guiding staff development programs, evaluating the performance of subordinate supervisors, and maintaining relationships with other organizational sections.

HOW TO TAKE A TEST

I. YOU MUST PASS AN EXAMINATION

A. WHAT EVERY CANDIDATE SHOULD KNOW

Examination applicants often ask us for help in preparing for the written test. What can I study in advance? What kinds of questions will be asked? How will the test be given? How will the papers be graded?

As an applicant for a civil service examination, you may be wondering about some of these things. Our purpose here is to suggest effective methods of advance study and to describe civil service examinations.

Your chances for success on this examination can be increased if you know how to prepare. Those "pre-examination jitters" can be reduced if you know what to expect. You can even experience an adventure in good citizenship if you know why civil service exams are given.

B. WHY ARE CIVIL SERVICE EXAMINATIONS GIVEN?

Civil service examinations are important to you in two ways. As a citizen, you want public jobs filled by employees who know how to do their work. As a job seeker, you want a fair chance to compete for that job on an equal footing with other candidates. The best-known means of accomplishing this two-fold goal is the competitive examination.

Exams are widely publicized throughout the nation. They may be administered for jobs in federal, state, city, municipal, town or village governments or agencies.

Any citizen may apply, with some limitations, such as the age or residence of applicants. Your experience and education may be reviewed to see whether you meet the requirements for the particular examination. When these requirements exist, they are reasonable and applied consistently to all applicants. Thus, a competitive examination may cause you some uneasiness now, but it is your privilege and safeguard.

C. HOW ARE CIVIL SERVICE EXAMS DEVELOPED?

Examinations are carefully written by trained technicians who are specialists in the field known as "psychological measurement," in consultation with recognized authorities in the field of work that the test will cover. These experts recommend the subject matter areas or skills to be tested; only those knowledges or skills important to your success on the job are included. The most reliable books and source materials available are used as references. Together, the experts and technicians judge the difficulty level of the questions.

Test technicians know how to phrase questions so that the problem is clearly stated. Their ethics do not permit "trick" or "catch" questions. Questions may have been tried out on sample groups, or subjected to statistical analysis, to determine their usefulness.

Written tests are often used in combination with performance tests, ratings of training and experience, and oral interviews. All of these measures combine to form the best-known means of finding the right person for the right job.

II. HOW TO PASS THE WRITTEN TEST

A. NATURE OF THE EXAMINATION

To prepare intelligently for civil service examinations, you should know how they differ from school examinations you have taken. In school you were assigned certain definite pages to read or subjects to cover. The examination questions were quite detailed and usually emphasized memory. Civil service exams, on the other hand, try to discover your present ability to perform the duties of a position, plus your potentiality to learn these duties. In other words, a civil service exam attempts to predict how successful you will be. Questions cover such a broad area that they cannot be as minute and detailed as school exam questions.

In the public service similar kinds of work, or positions, are grouped together in one "class." This process is known as *position-classification*. All the positions in a class are paid according to the salary range for that class. One class title covers all of these positions, and they are all tested by the same examination.

B. FOUR BASIC STEPS

1) Study the announcement

How, then, can you know what subjects to study? Our best answer is: "Learn as much as possible about the class of positions for which you've applied." The exam will test the knowledge, skills and abilities needed to do the work.

Your most valuable source of information about the position you want is the official exam announcement. This announcement lists the training and experience qualifications. Check these standards and apply only if you come reasonably close to meeting them.

The brief description of the position in the examination announcement offers some clues to the subjects which will be tested. Think about the job itself. Review the duties in your mind. Can you perform them, or are there some in which you are rusty? Fill in the blank spots in your preparation.

Many jurisdictions preview the written test in the exam announcement by including a section called "Knowledge and Abilities Required," "Scope of the Examination," or some similar heading. Here you will find out specifically what fields will be tested.

2) Review your own background

Once you learn in general what the position is all about, and what you need to know to do the work, ask yourself which subjects you already know fairly well and which need improvement. You may wonder whether to concentrate on improving your strong areas or on building some background in your fields of weakness. When the announcement has specified "some knowledge" or "considerable knowledge," or has used adjectives like "beginning principles of..." or "advanced ... methods," you can get a clue as to the number and difficulty of questions to be asked in any given field. More questions, and hence broader coverage, would be included for those subjects which are more important in the work. Now weigh your strengths and weaknesses against the job requirements and prepare accordingly.

3) Determine the level of the position

Another way to tell how intensively you should prepare is to understand the level of the job for which you are applying. Is it the entering level? In other words, is this the position in which beginners in a field of work are hired? Or is it an intermediate or advanced level? Sometimes this is indicated by such words as "Junior" or "Senior" in the class title. Other jurisdictions use Roman numerals to designate the level – Clerk I, Clerk II, for example. The word "Supervisor" sometimes appears in the title. If the level is not indicated by the title, check the description of duties. Will you be working under very close supervision, or will you have responsibility for independent decisions in this work?

4) Choose appropriate study materials

Now that you know the subjects to be examined and the relative amount of each subject to be covered, you can choose suitable study materials. For beginning level jobs, or even advanced ones, if you have a pronounced weakness in some aspect of your training, read a modern, standard textbook in that field. Be sure it is up to date and has general coverage. Such books are normally available at your library, and the librarian will be glad to help you locate one. For entry-level positions, questions of appropriate difficulty are chosen – neither highly advanced questions, nor those too simple. Such questions require careful thought but not advanced training.

If the position for which you are applying is technical or advanced, you will read more advanced, specialized material. If you are already familiar with the basic principles of your field, elementary textbooks would waste your time. Concentrate on advanced textbooks and technical periodicals. Think through the concepts and review difficult problems in your field.

These are all general sources. You can get more ideas on your own initiative, following these leads. For example, training manuals and publications of the government agency which employs workers in your field can be useful, particularly for technical and professional positions. A letter or visit to the government department involved may result in more specific study suggestions, and certainly will provide you with a more definite idea of the exact nature of the position you are seeking.

III. KINDS OF TESTS

Tests are used for purposes other than measuring knowledge and ability to perform specified duties. For some positions, it is equally important to test ability to make adjustments to new situations or to profit from training. In others, basic mental abilities not dependent on information are essential. Questions which test these things may not appear as pertinent to the duties of the position as those which test for knowledge and information. Yet they are often highly important parts of a fair examination. For very general questions, it is almost impossible to help you direct your study efforts. What we can do is to point out some of the more common of these general abilities needed in public service positions and describe some typical questions.

1) General information

Broad, general information has been found useful for predicting job success in some kinds of work. This is tested in a variety of ways, from vocabulary lists to questions about current events. Basic background in some field of work, such as sociology or economics, may be sampled in a group of questions. Often these are principles which have become familiar to most persons through exposure rather than through formal training. It is difficult to advise you how to study for these questions; being alert to the world around you is our best suggestion.

2) Verbal ability

An example of an ability needed in many positions is verbal or language ability. Verbal ability is, in brief, the ability to use and understand words. Vocabulary and grammar tests are typical measures of this ability. Reading comprehension or paragraph interpretation questions are common in many kinds of civil service tests. You are given a paragraph of written material and asked to find its central meaning.

3) Numerical ability

Number skills can be tested by the familiar arithmetic problem, by checking paired lists of numbers to see which are alike and which are different, or by interpreting charts and graphs. In the latter test, a graph may be printed in the test booklet which you are asked to use as the basis for answering questions.

4) Observation

A popular test for law-enforcement positions is the observation test. A picture is shown to you for several minutes, then taken away. Questions about the picture test your ability to observe both details and larger elements.

5) Following directions

In many positions in the public service, the employee must be able to carry out written instructions dependably and accurately. You may be given a chart with several columns, each column listing a variety of information. The questions require you to carry out directions involving the information given in the chart.

6) Skills and aptitudes

Performance tests effectively measure some manual skills and aptitudes. When the skill is one in which you are trained, such as typing or shorthand, you can practice. These tests are often very much like those given in business school or high school courses. For many of the other skills and aptitudes, however, no short-time preparation can be made. Skills and abilities natural to you or that you have developed throughout your lifetime are being tested.

Many of the general questions just described provide all the data needed to answer the questions and ask you to use your reasoning ability to find the answers. Your best preparation for these tests, as well as for tests of facts and ideas, is to be at your physical and mental best. You, no doubt, have your own methods of getting into an exam-taking mood and keeping "in shape." The next section lists some ideas on this subject.

IV. KINDS OF QUESTIONS

Only rarely is the "essay" question, which you answer in narrative form, used in civil service tests. Civil service tests are usually of the short-answer type. Full instructions for answering these questions will be given to you at the examination. But in case this is your first experience with short-answer questions and separate answer sheets, here is what you need to know:

1) Multiple-choice Questions

Most popular of the short-answer questions is the "multiple choice" or "best answer" question. It can be used, for example, to test for factual knowledge, ability to solve problems or judgment in meeting situations found at work.

A multiple-choice question is normally one of three types—
- It can begin with an incomplete statement followed by several possible endings. You are to find the one ending which *best* completes the statement, although some of the others may not be entirely wrong.
- It can also be a complete statement in the form of a question which is answered by choosing one of the statements listed.

- It can be in the form of a problem – again you select the best answer.

Here is an example of a multiple-choice question with a discussion which should give you some clues as to the method for choosing the right answer:

When an employee has a complaint about his assignment, the action which will *best* help him overcome his difficulty is to
   A. discuss his difficulty with his coworkers
   B. take the problem to the head of the organization
   C. take the problem to the person who gave him the assignment
   D. say nothing to anyone about his complaint

In answering this question, you should study each of the choices to find which is best. Consider choice "A" – Certainly an employee may discuss his complaint with fellow employees, but no change or improvement can result, and the complaint remains unresolved. Choice "B" is a poor choice since the head of the organization probably does not know what assignment you have been given, and taking your problem to him is known as "going over the head" of the supervisor. The supervisor, or person who made the assignment, is the person who can clarify it or correct any injustice. Choice "C" is, therefore, correct. To say nothing, as in choice "D," is unwise. Supervisors have and interest in knowing the problems employees are facing, and the employee is seeking a solution to his problem.

2) True/False Questions

The "true/false" or "right/wrong" form of question is sometimes used. Here a complete statement is given. Your job is to decide whether the statement is right or wrong.

SAMPLE: A roaming cell-phone call to a nearby city costs less than a non-roaming call to a distant city.

This statement is wrong, or false, since roaming calls are more expensive.

This is not a complete list of all possible question forms, although most of the others are variations of these common types. You will always get complete directions for answering questions. Be sure you understand *how* to mark your answers – ask questions until you do.

V. RECORDING YOUR ANSWERS

Computer terminals are used more and more today for many different kinds of exams.
For an examination with very few applicants, you may be told to record your answers in the test booklet itself. Separate answer sheets are much more common. If this separate answer sheet is to be scored by machine – and this is often the case – it is highly important that you mark your answers correctly in order to get credit.

An electronic scoring machine is often used in civil service offices because of the speed with which papers can be scored. Machine-scored answer sheets must be marked with a pencil, which will be given to you. This pencil has a high graphite content which responds to the electronic scoring machine. As a matter of fact, stray dots may register as answers, so do not let your pencil rest on the answer sheet while you are pondering the correct answer. Also, if your pencil lead breaks or is otherwise defective, ask for another.

Since the answer sheet will be dropped in a slot in the scoring machine, be careful not to bend the corners or get the paper crumpled.

The answer sheet normally has five vertical columns of numbers, with 30 numbers to a column. These numbers correspond to the question numbers in your test booklet. After each number, going across the page are four or five pairs of dotted lines. These short dotted lines have small letters or numbers above them. The first two pairs may also have a "T" or "F" above the letters. This indicates that the first two pairs only are to be used if the questions are of the true-false type. If the questions are multiple choice, disregard the "T" and "F" and pay attention only to the small letters or numbers.

Answer your questions in the manner of the sample that follows:

32. The largest city in the United States is
   A. Washington, D.C.
   B. New York City
   C. Chicago
   D. Detroit
   E. San Francisco

1) Choose the answer you think is best. (New York City is the largest, so "B" is correct.)
2) Find the row of dotted lines numbered the same as the question you are answering. (Find row number 32)
3) Find the pair of dotted lines corresponding to the answer. (Find the pair of lines under the mark "B.")
4) Make a solid black mark between the dotted lines.

VI. BEFORE THE TEST

Common sense will help you find procedures to follow to get ready for an examination. Too many of us, however, overlook these sensible measures. Indeed, nervousness and fatigue have been found to be the most serious reasons why applicants fail to do their best on civil service tests. Here is a list of reminders:

- Begin your preparation early – Don't wait until the last minute to go scurrying around for books and materials or to find out what the position is all about.
- Prepare continuously – An hour a night for a week is better than an all-night cram session. This has been definitely established. What is more, a night a week for a month will return better dividends than crowding your study into a shorter period of time.
- Locate the place of the exam – You have been sent a notice telling you when and where to report for the examination. If the location is in a different town or otherwise unfamiliar to you, it would be well to inquire the best route and learn something about the building.
- Relax the night before the test – Allow your mind to rest. Do not study at all that night. Plan some mild recreation or diversion; then go to bed early and get a good night's sleep.
- Get up early enough to make a leisurely trip to the place for the test – This way unforeseen events, traffic snarls, unfamiliar buildings, etc. will not upset you.
- Dress comfortably – A written test is not a fashion show. You will be known by number and not by name, so wear something comfortable.

- Leave excess paraphernalia at home – Shopping bags and odd bundles will get in your way. You need bring only the items mentioned in the official notice you received; usually everything you need is provided. Do not bring reference books to the exam. They will only confuse those last minutes and be taken away from you when in the test room.
- Arrive somewhat ahead of time – If because of transportation schedules you must get there very early, bring a newspaper or magazine to take your mind off yourself while waiting.
- Locate the examination room – When you have found the proper room, you will be directed to the seat or part of the room where you will sit. Sometimes you are given a sheet of instructions to read while you are waiting. Do not fill out any forms until you are told to do so; just read them and be prepared.
- Relax and prepare to listen to the instructions
- If you have any physical problem that may keep you from doing your best, be sure to tell the test administrator. If you are sick or in poor health, you really cannot do your best on the exam. You can come back and take the test some other time.

VII. AT THE TEST

The day of the test is here and you have the test booklet in your hand. The temptation to get going is very strong. Caution! There is more to success than knowing the right answers. You must know how to identify your papers and understand variations in the type of short-answer question used in this particular examination. Follow these suggestions for maximum results from your efforts:

1) Cooperate with the monitor

The test administrator has a duty to create a situation in which you can be as much at ease as possible. He will give instructions, tell you when to begin, check to see that you are marking your answer sheet correctly, and so on. He is not there to guard you, although he will see that your competitors do not take unfair advantage. He wants to help you do your best.

2) Listen to all instructions

Don't jump the gun! Wait until you understand all directions. In most civil service tests you get more time than you need to answer the questions. So don't be in a hurry. Read each word of instructions until you clearly understand the meaning. Study the examples, listen to all announcements and follow directions. Ask questions if you do not understand what to do.

3) Identify your papers

Civil service exams are usually identified by number only. You will be assigned a number; you must not put your name on your test papers. Be sure to copy your number correctly. Since more than one exam may be given, copy your exact examination title.

4) Plan your time

Unless you are told that a test is a "speed" or "rate of work" test, speed itself is usually not important. Time enough to answer all the questions will be provided, but this does not mean that you have all day. An overall time limit has been set. Divide the total time (in minutes) by the number of questions to determine the approximate time you have for each question.

5) Do not linger over difficult questions

If you come across a difficult question, mark it with a paper clip (useful to have along) and come back to it when you have been through the booklet. One caution if you do this – be sure to skip a number on your answer sheet as well. Check often to be sure that you have not lost your place and that you are marking in the row numbered the same as the question you are answering.

6) Read the questions

Be sure you know what the question asks! Many capable people are unsuccessful because they failed to *read* the questions correctly.

7) Answer all questions

Unless you have been instructed that a penalty will be deducted for incorrect answers, it is better to guess than to omit a question.

8) Speed tests

It is often better NOT to guess on speed tests. It has been found that on timed tests people are tempted to spend the last few seconds before time is called in marking answers at random – without even reading them – in the hope of picking up a few extra points. To discourage this practice, the instructions may warn you that your score will be "corrected" for guessing. That is, a penalty will be applied. The incorrect answers will be deducted from the correct ones, or some other penalty formula will be used.

9) Review your answers

If you finish before time is called, go back to the questions you guessed or omitted to give them further thought. Review other answers if you have time.

10) Return your test materials

If you are ready to leave before others have finished or time is called, take ALL your materials to the monitor and leave quietly. Never take any test material with you. The monitor can discover whose papers are not complete, and taking a test booklet may be grounds for disqualification.

VIII. EXAMINATION TECHNIQUES

1) Read the general instructions carefully. These are usually printed on the first page of the exam booklet. As a rule, these instructions refer to the timing of the examination; the fact that you should not start work until the signal and must stop work at a signal, etc. If there are any *special* instructions, such as a choice of questions to be answered, make sure that you note this instruction carefully.

2) When you are ready to start work on the examination, that is as soon as the signal has been given, read the instructions to each question booklet, underline any key words or phrases, such as *least, best, outline, describe* and the like. In this way you will tend to answer as requested rather than discover on reviewing your paper that you *listed without describing*, that you selected the *worst* choice rather than the *best* choice, etc.

3) If the examination is of the objective or multiple-choice type – that is, each question will also give a series of possible answers: A, B, C or D, and you are called upon to select the best answer and write the letter next to that answer on your answer paper – it is advisable to start answering each question in turn. There may be anywhere from 50 to 100 such questions in the three or four hours allotted and you can see how much time would be taken if you read through all the questions before beginning to answer any. Furthermore, if you come across a question or group of questions which you know would be difficult to answer, it would undoubtedly affect your handling of all the other questions.

4) If the examination is of the essay type and contains but a few questions, it is a moot point as to whether you should read all the questions before starting to answer any one. Of course, if you are given a choice – say five out of seven and the like – then it is essential to read all the questions so you can eliminate the two that are most difficult. If, however, you are asked to answer all the questions, there may be danger in trying to answer the easiest one first because you may find that you will spend too much time on it. The best technique is to answer the first question, then proceed to the second, etc.

5) Time your answers. Before the exam begins, write down the time it started, then add the time allowed for the examination and write down the time it must be completed, then divide the time available somewhat as follows:
   - If 3-1/2 hours are allowed, that would be 210 minutes. If you have 80 objective-type questions, that would be an average of 2-1/2 minutes per question. Allow yourself no more than 2 minutes per question, or a total of 160 minutes, which will permit about 50 minutes to review.
   - If for the time allotment of 210 minutes there are 7 essay questions to answer, that would average about 30 minutes a question. Give yourself only 25 minutes per question so that you have about 35 minutes to review.

6) The most important instruction is to *read each question* and make sure you know what is wanted. The second most important instruction is to *time yourself properly* so that you answer every question. The third most important instruction is to *answer every question*. Guess if you have to but include something for each question. Remember that you will receive no credit for a blank and will probably receive some credit if you write something in answer to an essay question. If you guess a letter – say "B" for a multiple-choice question – you may have guessed right. If you leave a blank as an answer to a multiple-choice question, the examiners may respect your feelings but it will not add a point to your score. Some exams may penalize you for wrong answers, so in such cases *only*, you may not want to guess unless you have some basis for your answer.

7) Suggestions
   a. Objective-type questions
      1. Examine the question booklet for proper sequence of pages and questions
      2. Read all instructions carefully
      3. Skip any question which seems too difficult; return to it after all other questions have been answered
      4. Apportion your time properly; do not spend too much time on any single question or group of questions

5. Note and underline key words – *all, most, fewest, least, best, worst, same, opposite*, etc.
6. Pay particular attention to negatives
7. Note unusual option, e.g., unduly long, short, complex, different or similar in content to the body of the question
8. Observe the use of "hedging" words – *probably, may, most likely*, etc.
9. Make sure that your answer is put next to the same number as the question
10. Do not second-guess unless you have good reason to believe the second answer is definitely more correct
11. Cross out original answer if you decide another answer is more accurate; do not erase until you are ready to hand your paper in
12. Answer all questions; guess unless instructed otherwise
13. Leave time for review

   b. Essay questions
1. Read each question carefully
2. Determine exactly what is wanted. Underline key words or phrases.
3. Decide on outline or paragraph answer
4. Include many different points and elements unless asked to develop any one or two points or elements
5. Show impartiality by giving pros and cons unless directed to select one side only
6. Make and write down any assumptions you find necessary to answer the questions
7. Watch your English, grammar, punctuation and choice of words
8. Time your answers; don't crowd material

8) Answering the essay question

Most essay questions can be answered by framing the specific response around several key words or ideas. Here are a few such key words or ideas:

M's: manpower, materials, methods, money, management
P's: purpose, program, policy, plan, procedure, practice, problems, pitfalls, personnel, public relations

   a. Six basic steps in handling problems:
1. Preliminary plan and background development
2. Collect information, data and facts
3. Analyze and interpret information, data and facts
4. Analyze and develop solutions as well as make recommendations
5. Prepare report and sell recommendations
6. Install recommendations and follow up effectiveness

   b. Pitfalls to avoid
1. *Taking things for granted* – A statement of the situation does not necessarily imply that each of the elements is necessarily true; for example, a complaint may be invalid and biased so that all that can be taken for granted is that a complaint has been registered

2. *Considering only one side of a situation* – Wherever possible, indicate several alternatives and then point out the reasons you selected the best one
3. *Failing to indicate follow up* – Whenever your answer indicates action on your part, make certain that you will take proper follow-up action to see how successful your recommendations, procedures or actions turn out to be
4. *Taking too long in answering any single question* – Remember to time your answers properly

IX. AFTER THE TEST

Scoring procedures differ in detail among civil service jurisdictions although the general principles are the same. Whether the papers are hand-scored or graded by machine we have described, they are nearly always graded by number. That is, the person who marks the paper knows only the number – never the name – of the applicant. Not until all the papers have been graded will they be matched with names. If other tests, such as training and experience or oral interview ratings have been given, scores will be combined. Different parts of the examination usually have different weights. For example, the written test might count 60 percent of the final grade, and a rating of training and experience 40 percent. In many jurisdictions, veterans will have a certain number of points added to their grades.

After the final grade has been determined, the names are placed in grade order and an eligible list is established. There are various methods for resolving ties between those who get the same final grade – probably the most common is to place first the name of the person whose application was received first. Job offers are made from the eligible list in the order the names appear on it. You will be notified of your grade and your rank as soon as all these computations have been made. This will be done as rapidly as possible.

People who are found to meet the requirements in the announcement are called "eligibles." Their names are put on a list of eligible candidates. An eligible's chances of getting a job depend on how high he stands on this list and how fast agencies are filling jobs from the list.

When a job is to be filled from a list of eligibles, the agency asks for the names of people on the list of eligibles for that job. When the civil service commission receives this request, it sends to the agency the names of the three people highest on this list. Or, if the job to be filled has specialized requirements, the office sends the agency the names of the top three persons who meet these requirements from the general list.

The appointing officer makes a choice from among the three people whose names were sent to him. If the selected person accepts the appointment, the names of the others are put back on the list to be considered for future openings.

That is the rule in hiring from all kinds of eligible lists, whether they are for typist, carpenter, chemist, or something else. For every vacancy, the appointing officer has his choice of any one of the top three eligibles on the list. This explains why the person whose name is on top of the list sometimes does not get an appointment when some of the persons lower on the list do. If the appointing officer chooses the second or third eligible, the No. 1 eligible does not get a job at once, but stays on the list until he is appointed or the list is terminated.

X. HOW TO PASS THE INTERVIEW TEST

The examination for which you applied requires an oral interview test. You have already taken the written test and you are now being called for the interview test – the final part of the formal examination.

You may think that it is not possible to prepare for an interview test and that there are no procedures to follow during an interview. Our purpose is to point out some things you can do in advance that will help you and some good rules to follow and pitfalls to avoid while you are being interviewed.

What is an interview supposed to test?

The written examination is designed to test the technical knowledge and competence of the candidate; the oral is designed to evaluate intangible qualities, not readily measured otherwise, and to establish a list showing the relative fitness of each candidate – as measured against his competitors – for the position sought. Scoring is not on the basis of "right" and "wrong," but on a sliding scale of values ranging from "not passable" to "outstanding." As a matter of fact, it is possible to achieve a relatively low score without a single "incorrect" answer because of evident weakness in the qualities being measured.

Occasionally, an examination may consist entirely of an oral test – either an individual or a group oral. In such cases, information is sought concerning the technical knowledges and abilities of the candidate, since there has been no written examination for this purpose. More commonly, however, an oral test is used to supplement a written examination.

Who conducts interviews?

The composition of oral boards varies among different jurisdictions. In nearly all, a representative of the personnel department serves as chairman. One of the members of the board may be a representative of the department in which the candidate would work. In some cases, "outside experts" are used, and, frequently, a businessman or some other representative of the general public is asked to serve. Labor and management or other special groups may be represented. The aim is to secure the services of experts in the appropriate field.

However the board is composed, it is a good idea (and not at all improper or unethical) to ascertain in advance of the interview who the members are and what groups they represent. When you are introduced to them, you will have some idea of their backgrounds and interests, and at least you will not stutter and stammer over their names.

What should be done before the interview?

While knowledge about the board members is useful and takes some of the surprise element out of the interview, there is other preparation which is more substantive. It *is* possible to prepare for an oral interview – in several ways:

1) Keep a copy of your application and review it carefully before the interview

This may be the only document before the oral board, and the starting point of the interview. Know what education and experience you have listed there, and the sequence and dates of all of it. Sometimes the board will ask you to review the highlights of your experience for them; you should not have to hem and haw doing it.

2) Study the class specification and the examination announcement

Usually, the oral board has one or both of these to guide them. The qualities, characteristics or knowledges required by the position sought are stated in these documents. They offer valuable clues as to the nature of the oral interview. For example, if the job involves supervisory responsibilities, the announcement will usually indicate that knowledge of modern supervisory methods and the qualifications of the candidate as a supervisor will be tested. If so, you can expect such questions, frequently in the form of a hypothetical situation which you are expected to solve. NEVER go into an oral without knowledge of the duties and responsibilities of the job you seek.

3) Think through each qualification required

Try to visualize the kind of questions you would ask if you were a board member. How well could you answer them? Try especially to appraise your own knowledge and background in each area, *measured against the job sought*, and identify any areas in which you are weak. Be critical and realistic – do not flatter yourself.

4) Do some general reading in areas in which you feel you may be weak

For example, if the job involves supervision and your past experience has NOT, some general reading in supervisory methods and practices, particularly in the field of human relations, might be useful. Do NOT study agency procedures or detailed manuals. The oral board will be testing your understanding and capacity, not your memory.

5) Get a good night's sleep and watch your general health and mental attitude

You will want a clear head at the interview. Take care of a cold or any other minor ailment, and of course, no hangovers.

What should be done on the day of the interview?

Now comes the day of the interview itself. Give yourself plenty of time to get there. Plan to arrive somewhat ahead of the scheduled time, particularly if your appointment is in the fore part of the day. If a previous candidate fails to appear, the board might be ready for you a bit early. By early afternoon an oral board is almost invariably behind schedule if there are many candidates, and you may have to wait. Take along a book or magazine to read, or your application to review, but leave any extraneous material in the waiting room when you go in for your interview. In any event, relax and compose yourself.

The matter of dress is important. The board is forming impressions about you – from your experience, your manners, your attitude, and your appearance. Give your personal appearance careful attention. Dress your best, but not your flashiest. Choose conservative, appropriate clothing, and be sure it is immaculate. This is a business interview, and your appearance should indicate that you regard it as such. Besides, being well groomed and properly dressed will help boost your confidence.

Sooner or later, someone will call your name and escort you into the interview room. *This is it.* From here on you are on your own. It is too late for any more preparation. But remember, you asked for this opportunity to prove your fitness, and you are here because your request was granted.

What happens when you go in?

The usual sequence of events will be as follows: The clerk (who is often the board stenographer) will introduce you to the chairman of the oral board, who will introduce you to the other members of the board. Acknowledge the introductions before you sit down. Do not be surprised if you find a microphone facing you or a stenotypist sitting by. Oral interviews are usually recorded in the event of an appeal or other review.

Usually the chairman of the board will open the interview by reviewing the highlights of your education and work experience from your application – primarily for the benefit of the other members of the board, as well as to get the material into the record. Do not interrupt or comment unless there is an error or significant misinterpretation; if that is the case, do not hesitate. But do not quibble about insignificant matters. Also, he will usually ask you some question about your education, experience or your present job – partly to get you to start talking and to establish the interviewing "rapport." He may start the actual questioning, or turn it over to one of the other members. Frequently, each member undertakes the questioning on a particular area, one in which he is perhaps most competent, so you can expect each member to participate in the examination. Because time is limited, you may also expect some rather abrupt switches in the direction the questioning takes, so do not be upset by it. Normally, a board member will not pursue a single line of questioning unless he discovers a particular strength or weakness.

After each member has participated, the chairman will usually ask whether any member has any further questions, then will ask you if you have anything you wish to add. Unless you are expecting this question, it may floor you. Worse, it may start you off on an extended, extemporaneous speech. The board is not usually seeking more information. The question is principally to offer you a last opportunity to present further qualifications or to indicate that you have nothing to add. So, if you feel that a significant qualification or characteristic has been overlooked, it is proper to point it out in a sentence or so. Do not compliment the board on the thoroughness of their examination – they have been sketchy, and you know it. If you wish, merely say, "No thank you, I have nothing further to add." This is a point where you can "talk yourself out" of a good impression or fail to present an important bit of information. Remember, *you close the interview yourself.*

The chairman will then say, "That is all, Mr. _____, thank you." Do not be startled; the interview is over, and quicker than you think. Thank him, gather your belongings and take your leave. Save your sigh of relief for the other side of the door.

How to put your best foot forward

Throughout this entire process, you may feel that the board individually and collectively is trying to pierce your defenses, seek out your hidden weaknesses and embarrass and confuse you. Actually, this is not true. They are obliged to make an appraisal of your qualifications for the job you are seeking, and they want to see you in your best light. Remember, they must interview all candidates and a non-cooperative candidate may become a failure in spite of their best efforts to bring out his qualifications. Here are 15 suggestions that will help you:

1) Be natural – Keep your attitude confident, not cocky

If you are not confident that you can do the job, do not expect the board to be. Do not apologize for your weaknesses, try to bring out your strong points. The board is interested in a positive, not negative, presentation. Cockiness will antagonize any board member and make him wonder if you are covering up a weakness by a false show of strength.

2) Get comfortable, but don't lounge or sprawl

Sit erectly but not stiffly. A careless posture may lead the board to conclude that you are careless in other things, or at least that you are not impressed by the importance of the occasion. Either conclusion is natural, even if incorrect. Do not fuss with your clothing, a pencil or an ashtray. Your hands may occasionally be useful to emphasize a point; do not let them become a point of distraction.

3) Do not wisecrack or make small talk

This is a serious situation, and your attitude should show that you consider it as such. Further, the time of the board is limited – they do not want to waste it, and neither should you.

4) Do not exaggerate your experience or abilities
In the first place, from information in the application or other interviews and sources, the board may know more about you than you think. Secondly, you probably will not get away with it. An experienced board is rather adept at spotting such a situation, so do not take the chance.

5) If you know a board member, do not make a point of it, yet do not hide it
Certainly you are not fooling him, and probably not the other members of the board. Do not try to take advantage of your acquaintanceship – it will probably do you little good.

6) Do not dominate the interview
Let the board do that. They will give you the clues – do not assume that you have to do all the talking. Realize that the board has a number of questions to ask you, and do not try to take up all the interview time by showing off your extensive knowledge of the answer to the first one.

7) Be attentive
You only have 20 minutes or so, and you should keep your attention at its sharpest throughout. When a member is addressing a problem or question to you, give him your undivided attention. Address your reply principally to him, but do not exclude the other board members.

8) Do not interrupt
A board member may be stating a problem for you to analyze. He will ask you a question when the time comes. Let him state the problem, and wait for the question.

9) Make sure you understand the question
Do not try to answer until you are sure what the question is. If it is not clear, restate it in your own words or ask the board member to clarify it for you. However, do not haggle about minor elements.

10) Reply promptly but not hastily
A common entry on oral board rating sheets is "candidate responded readily," or "candidate hesitated in replies." Respond as promptly and quickly as you can, but do not jump to a hasty, ill-considered answer.

11) Do not be peremptory in your answers
A brief answer is proper – but do not fire your answer back. That is a losing game from your point of view. The board member can probably ask questions much faster than you can answer them.

12) Do not try to create the answer you think the board member wants
He is interested in what kind of mind you have and how it works – not in playing games. Furthermore, he can usually spot this practice and will actually grade you down on it.

13) Do not switch sides in your reply merely to agree with a board member
Frequently, a member will take a contrary position merely to draw you out and to see if you are willing and able to defend your point of view. Do not start a debate, yet do not surrender a good position. If a position is worth taking, it is worth defending.

14) Do not be afraid to admit an error in judgment if you are shown to be wrong

The board knows that you are forced to reply without any opportunity for careful consideration. Your answer may be demonstrably wrong. If so, admit it and get on with the interview.

15) Do not dwell at length on your present job

The opening question may relate to your present assignment. Answer the question but do not go into an extended discussion. You are being examined for a *new* job, not your present one. As a matter of fact, try to phrase ALL your answers in terms of the job for which you are being examined.

Basis of Rating

Probably you will forget most of these "do's" and "don'ts" when you walk into the oral interview room. Even remembering them all will not ensure you a passing grade. Perhaps you did not have the qualifications in the first place. But remembering them will help you to put your best foot forward, without treading on the toes of the board members.

Rumor and popular opinion to the contrary notwithstanding, an oral board wants you to make the best appearance possible. They know you are under pressure – but they also want to see how you respond to it as a guide to what your reaction would be under the pressures of the job you seek. They will be influenced by the degree of poise you display, the personal traits you show and the manner in which you respond.

ABOUT THIS BOOK

This book contains tests divided into Examination Sections. Go through each test, answering every question in the margin. We have also attached a sample answer sheet at the back of the book that can be removed and used. At the end of each test look at the answer key and check your answers. On the ones you got wrong, look at the right answer choice and learn. Do not fill in the answers first. Do not memorize the questions and answers, but understand the answer and principles involved. On your test, the questions will likely be different from the samples. Questions are changed and new ones added. If you understand these past questions you should have success with any changes that arise. Tests may consist of several types of questions. We have additional books on each subject should more study be advisable or necessary for you. Finally, the more you study, the better prepared you will be. This book is intended to be the last thing you study before you walk into the examination room. Prior study of relevant texts is also recommended. NLC publishes some of these in our Fundamental Series. Knowledge and good sense are important factors in passing your exam. Good luck also helps. So now study this Passbook, absorb the material contained within and take that knowledge into the examination. Then do your best to pass that exam.

EXAMINATION SECTION

SAMPLE TEST

PRINCIPLES AND PRACTICES OF PROGRAM PLANNING AND PROJECT MANAGEMENT

Test material will be presented in a multiple-choice question format.

Test Task: You will be presented with situations in which you must apply knowledge of program planning and project management in order to answer the questions correctly.

SAMPLE QUESTION:
Which one of the following is developed by the project manager to clearly define the boundaries of a project by detailing the product, deliverables, and major objectives?

- A. cost baseline
- B. scope statement
- C. risk management plan
- D. quality management plan

The correct answer to this sample question is Choice B.

Solution:

Choice A is not correct. A cost baseline is a time-phased budget that a project manager prepares to monitor and measure cost performance throughout the project life cycle. It does not define the product, deliverables, or major objectives of the project.

Choice B is the correct answer to this question. The scope statement is developed by the project manager to define the project boundaries by outlining the product, deliverables, and major objectives.

Choice C is not correct. A risk management plan is a document that a project manager prepares to foresee risks, estimate impacts, and define responses to issues. It does not define the product, deliverables, or major objectives of the project.

Choice D is not correct. A quality management plan is a document that a project manager prepares to define the acceptable level of quality, which is typically defined by the customer, and to describe how the project will ensure this level of quality in its deliverables and work processes. It does not define the product, deliverables, or major objectives of the project.

EXAMINATION SECTION
TEST 1

DIRECTIONS: Each question or incomplete statement is followed by several suggested answers or completions. Select the one that BEST answers the question or completes the statement. *PRINT THE LETTER OF THE CORRECT ANSWER IN THE SPACE AT THE RIGHT.*

1. _____ is commonly used to report on project performance.
    A. Earned Value Management
    B. WBS
    C. Quality Management Plan
    D. RBS

2. Which of the following is NOT a process associated with communications management?
    A. Distribute information
    B. Manage stakeholder expectations
    C. Plan communication
    D. Survey questionnaire

3. As a project manager, you are expected to make relevant information available to project stakeholders as planned. Which process does this relate to?
    A. Distribute information
    B. Manage stakeholder expectations
    C. Plan communication
    D. Report performance

4. Report performance involves all of the following EXCEPT
    A. collecting and distributing performance data
    B. collecting and distributing progress measurements
    C. collecting stakeholder information needs
    D. collecting and distributing forecasts

5. Of the following examples listed, which is a sign of feedback from the receiver?
    A. No written response from the receiver
    B. An acknowledgement or additional questions from the receiver
    C. Encoding the message by the receiver
    D. Decoding the message by the receiver

6. As a project manager you are expected to create a scope statement. Once you have the statement, you find it to be useful in all the following ways EXCEPT
    A. describing the purpose of the project
    B. describing the objectives of the project
    C. distributing information
    D. explaining the business problems the project is expected to solve

7. What are project deliverables?
   A. Tangible products that the project is expected to deliver
   B. Prioritized list of deliverables
   C. Project scope statement
   D. Project documents

8. As a project manager, you are arranging criteria for project completion criteria. You could organize it using all of the following EXCEPT
   A. functional department
   B. milestones
   C. tasks of projects
   D. project phase

9. Which of the following is not a task under "Developing human resource plan"?
   A. Documenting organizational relationships
   B. Looking for the availability of required human resources
   C. Identification and documentation of project roles and responsibilities
   D. Creating a staffing plan

10. If you are a project manager who is keen in managing a project team, you would undertake any of the following EXCEPT
    A. creating a staffing plan
    B. evaluating individual team member performance
    C. providing feedback
    D. resolving conflicts

11. Nurturing the team is a vital role of a project manager. If you have to do so, what would you avoid?
    A. Guide the team members as required
    B. Provide mentoring throughout the project
    C. Remove the team member who is found to be less skilled
    D. On-the-job training

12. War room creation is an example of
    A. co-location
    B. management skills
    C. rewards and recognitions
    D. establishing ground rules

13. The team member roles and responsibilities could be documented using all of the following EXCEPT
    A. functional chart
    B. text-oriented format
    C. hierarchical type organizational chart
    D. matrix-based responsibility chart

14. _____ is NOT an example of constraints placed upon the project by current organizational policies.
    A. Hiring freeze
    B. Reduced training funds
    C. Organizational chart templates
    D. Rewards and Increments Freeze

15. As a project manager, you have decided to have a virtual team. What kind of limitation would this create with regards to team development?
    A. Rewards and recognition
    B. Establishing ground rules
    C. Team building
    D. Co-location

16. Unplanned training means
    A. team building using virtual team arrangement
    B. competencies developed as a result of project performance appraisals
    C. on-the-job training
    D. training that is done without any planning in advance

17. Resource break down structure is an example of
    A. functional chart
    B. text-oriented format
    C. hierarchical type organizational chart
    D. matrix-based responsibility chart

18. A project manager would consider the following as inputs to define scope EXCEPT
    A. requirements document
    B. project Charter
    C. product management plan
    D. organizational process charts

19. Aldo is a project manager and has to terminate a project earlier than planned. The level and extent of completion should be documented. Under which is this done?
    A. Verify scope
    B. Create scope
    C. Control scope
    D. Define scope

20. Sam, an IT project manager, is having difficulty in getting resources for his project, and hence has to depend highly on department heads. Which type of organization is Sam most likely working with?
    A. Functional
    B. Tight matrix
    C. Weak matrix
    D. Projectized

Questions 21-25.

Len is a project manager of an infrastructure project manager of a well-known company. He is involved in various processes of scope management. Look at the following chart and align the different processes to various tasks listed. Choose the appropriate answer for each process and list them under corresponding tasks.

	Processes	Corresponding tasks	List of tasks
21.	Define scope	21._____	A. Monitoring project scope and project status
22.	Control scope	22._____	B. Defining and documenting stakeholder needs
23.	Collect requirements	23._____	C. Formalizing acceptance of the complete project deliverables
24.	Verify scope	24._____	D. Breaking down the project into smaller, more manageable tasks
25.	Create WBS	25._____	E. Developing a detailed description of the project and its ultimate product

---

KEY (CORRECT ANSWERS)

1. A
2. D
3. A
4. C
5. B

6. C
7. A
8. C
9. B
10. A

11. C
12. A
13. A
14. C
15. D

16. B
17. C
18. C
19. A
20. A

21. E
22. A
23. B
24. C
25. D

TEST 2

DIRECTIONS: Each question or incomplete statement is followed by several suggested answers or completions. Select the one that BEST answers the question or completes the statement. *PRINT THE LETTER OF THE CORRECT ANSWER IN THE SPACE AT THE RIGHT.*

1. In which of the following processes would risk be identified? 1.____
    A. Risk identification
    B. Risk monitoring and control
    C. Qualitative risk analysis
    D. Risk identification, monitoring and control

2. Jack has prepared a risk management plan for his project and also identified risks in his project. Which of the following processes should Jack do next? 2.____
    A. Plan risk responses
    B. Perform qualitative analysis
    C. Perform quantitative analysis
    D. Monitor and control risk

3. Which of the following is NOT a step in risk management? 3.____
    A. Perform qualitative analysis
    B. Monitor and control risk
    C. Risk identification
    D. Risk breakdown structure

4. Sue is a project manager for an IT project at a corporate office. She is engaged in the process of identifying risks. To do so, she collects inputs from experts from the field through a questionnaire. What is this technique called? 4.____
    A. Interview
    B. Documentation review
    C. Delphi technique
    D. Register risk

5. Positive risks may be responded by which of the following: 5.____
    I. Exploit   II. Accept   III. Mitigate   IV. Share

    A. I and III
    B. All of the above
    C. I, II and IV
    D. I, II and III

6. Risk _____ is a response to negative risks. 6.____
    A. identification
    B. mitigation
    C. response plan
    D. management plan

7

7. Which of the following statements is NOT true about risk management?
    A. Risk register documents all the risks in detail
    B. Risks always have negative impacts and not positive
    C. Risk mitigation is a response to negative risks
    D. Risk register documents the risks in detail

8. _____ is the document that lists all the risks in a hierarchical fashion.
    A. Risk breakdown structure
    B. Lists of risks
    C. Risk management plan
    D. Monte Carlo diagram

9. Nicole is a project manager of a reforestation project. In one of the project reviews, she realizes that a risk has occurred. Which document should Nicole refer to take an appropriate action?
    A. Risk response plan
    B. Risk register
    C. Risk management plan
    D. Risk breakdown structure

10. As a project manager, you have invited experts for an effective brainstorming session to identify risks involved in the project. What is the ideal group size?
    A. 3   B. 6   C. 4   D. 5

11. Of the following personnel, who is NOT involved in project risk identification activities?
    A. Clerical staff
    B. Subject matter experts
    C. Other project managers
    D. Risk management experts

12. _____ is one of the tools/techniques used in risk identification.
    A. Risk tracker
    B. Checklist analysis
    C. Risk register
    D. Project scope

13. Jim is a project manager in a bank. He is collecting input for the risk identification process. What input would he be collecting to identify risks?
    I. Project scope statement
    II. Enterprise environmental factors
    III. Project management plan
    IV. Diagramming techniques

    A. I and IV only
    B. III and IV only
    C. All of the above
    D. I, II and III only

14. Which of the following could a project manager collect from a risk tracker?
    I. Root causes of risk and updated risk categories
    II. List of identified risks
    III. Risk register
    IV. List of potential responses

    A. I and IV only
    B. III and IV only
    C. I, II and IV
    D. II only

15. The risk management plan should describe the entire risk management process, including auditing of the process, and should also define _____.
    A. reporting
    B. environmental factors
    C. organizational process assets
    D. project management plan

16. What do risk categories define?
    A. How to communicate risk activities and their results
    B. Types and sources of risks
    C. How risk management will be done on the process
    D. When and how the risk management activities appear in the project schedule

17. Which of the following is not a method of risk identification?
    A. Diagramming
    B. Interviewing
    C. SWOT
    D. RBS

18. Shauna is conducting a qualitative risk analysis for her project. What is she required to do?
    A. Apply a numerical rating to each risk
    B. Assess the probability and impact of each identified risk
    C. Assign each major risk to a risk owner
    D. Outline a course of action for each major risk identified

19. Which of the following is not a criterion to close a risk?
    A. Risk is no longer valid
    B. Risk event has occurred
    C. Risk activities are recorded regularly
    D. Risk closure at the direction of a project manager

20. As a project manager, you establish a risk contingency budget. Which of the following is not a purpose of establishing a risk contingency budget?
    A. To be reviewed as a standing agenda item for project team meetings
    B. To prepare in advance to manage the risks successfully
    C. To have some reserve funds
    D. To avoid going over the budget allotted

20._____

21. Which of the following statements is NOT correct in terms of designing a risk management?
    A. Risk is inherent to project work
    B. In any organization, projects will have common risks
    C. Some risks may occur more than once in the life a project
    D. Risks identified will definitely occur

21._____

22. All identified potential risk events that are viewed to be relevant to the project are to be recorded using the
    A. risk register
    B. risk management matrix
    C. risk report
    D. SOW

22._____

23. _____ is/are an example of a business risk.
    A. Poorly understood requirements
    B. A merger
    C. Introduction of new technology to the organization
    D. Work outside the project scope

23._____

24. Personnel turnover in a project is a
    A. Business risk
    B. Not a risk at all
    C. Technology risk
    D. Project risk

24._____

25. Which of the following is not an example of mitigation?
    A. Set expectations
    B. Involve customer in early planning process
    C. Provide training for personnel
    D. Hiring a backup person for a key team member

25._____

KEY (CORRECT ANSWERS)

1. D
2. B
3. D
4. C
5. C

6. B
7. B
8. A
9. A
10. A

11. A
12. B
13. D
14. C
15. A

16. B
17. D
18. B
19. C
20. A

21. D
22. B
23. B
24. D
25. D

TEST 3

DIRECTIONS: Each question or incomplete statement is followed by several suggested answers of completions. Select the one that best answers the question or complete the statement. *PRINT THE LETTER OF THE CORRECT ANSWER IN THE SPACE AT THE RIGHT.*

1. Project cost management deals with all the following EXCEPT:
   A. Estimating costs
   B. Budgeting
   C. Controlling costs
   D. Communicating costs

2. Which of the following is not a process associated with project cost management?
   A. Control costs
   B. Maintain reserves
   C. Estimate costs
   D. Determine budget

3. _____ is not a key deliverable of project cost processes.
   A. Cost performance baseline
   B. Activity cost estimates
   C. Results of estimates
   D. Work performance measurements

4. As a project manager, you are calculating depreciation for an object. You are doing this by depreciating the same amount from the cost each year.
   What kind of depreciation technique are you applying?
   A. Sum of year depreciation
   B. Double-declining balance
   C. Multiple depreciation
   D. Straight line depreciation

5. Which of the following is not a characteristic of analogous estimating?
   A. It is a top-down approach
   B. It is a form of an expert judgment
   C. It makes less time when compared to bottom-up estimation
   D. It is more accurate when compared to bottom-up estimation

6. CPI = EV/AC. If CPI is less than 1, the project
   A. is over the budget
   B. is within the budget
   C. would be left over with unused budget
   D. efficiency is less

7. Which of the following is not a tool used for estimating cost?
   A. Cost of quality
   B. Expert judgment
   C. Two point estimates
   D. Three point estimates

8. What are the traditional project management triple constraints?
   A. Time, cost, resources
   B. Scope, cost, resources
   C. Scope, time, cost
   D. Resources, scope, budget

9. Sam, an IT project manager, is having difficulty getting resources for his project, and hence has to depend highly on department heads.
   Which type of organization is Sam most likely working with?
   A. Functional
   B. Tight Matrix
   C. Weak Matrix
   D. Projectized

9._____

10. After-project costs are called _____.
    A. cost of quality
    B. extra costs
    C. life cycle costs
    D. over budget costs

10._____

11. Critical chain is a tool and technique for _____.
    A. developing schedule process
    B. defining critical path
    C. sequencing activities process
    D. estimating activity duration

11._____

12. The following are outputs for sequencing activities:
    A. Project schedule network diagram, Milestone list
    B. Project document updates, Project schedule network diagram
    C. Project schedule, Project document updates
    D. Schedule data, Schedule baseline

12._____

13. The schedule performance index is a measure of:
    A. Difference between earned value and planned value
    B. Ratio between earned value and planned value
    C. Difference between earned value and estimate at completion
    D. Ratio between estimate at completion and earned value

13._____

14. Which of the following is not an input, output or tools and technique for control schedule process?
    A. Project schedule, work performance measurements and variance analysis
    B. Project management plan, project document updates and schedule compression
    C. Work performance information, schedule baseline and schedule data
    D. Project schedule, change requests and resource leveling

14._____

15. Contracts, resource calendar, risk register and forecasts are all termed as
    A. inputs to administer procurements process
    B. outputs from close procurements process
    C. project documents
    D. tools and techniques of conduct procurement process

15._____

16. Fast tracking can be best described as
    A. one of the schedule compression techniques
    B. adding resources to activities on critical path
    C. shared or critical resources available only at specific times
    D. performing activities in parallel to shorten project duration

16._____

17. Which of the following contract types places the highest risk on the seller?
    A. Cost plus fixed fee
    B. Firm fixed price
    C. Cost plus incentive fee
    D. Time and material

18. Using the Power/Interest grid, a stakeholder with low power and having high interest on the project should be
    A. monitored
    B. managed closely
    C. kept satisfied
    D. kept informed

19. Stakeholder classification information is found in which of the following documents?
    A. Communications management plan
    B. Stakeholder register
    C. Stakeholder management strategy document
    D. Human resource plan

20. Thomas is a project manager of a well-reputed organization. One of your senior managers approaches you to explain constraints on labor utilization followed by a request to delay a couple of your projects. What is the best way to approach this situation?
    A. Agree with the senior manager and delay a couple of your projects
    B. Perform an impact analysis of the requested change
    C. Report the situation to the senior management and make a complaint against the senior manager
    D. Disagree with the senior manager and continue with the progress of the projects managed by you

21. Project management is defined as
    A. completion of a project
    B. gaining trust of the people involved in the project
    C. completing a WBS
    D. the application of specific knowledge, skills and tools

22. The most common form of dependency is
    A. Start to Start
    B. Finish to Start
    C. Finish to Finish
    D. Start to Finish

23. Kelly is a project manager who is in phase of project evaluation. Which of the following has to be considered during project evaluation phase?
    I. Give feedback to team members
    II. Learn from experiences
    III. Monitor
    IV. Celebrate

The correct answer(s) is/are:
A. I only
B. I, IV and III
C. III only
D. I, II and IV

24. Which of the following are very vital for the implementation of the project, and also must be repeated over and over during project's life.
    I. Correct
    II. Monitor
    III. Estimate time and cost
    IV. Analyze

    The correct answer(s) is/are:
    A. I, II and III
    B. III only
    C. I, III and IV
    D. I, II and IV

25. What is the average amount of time is to be allocated to project planning?
    A. 10%
    B. 25%
    C. 22%
    D. 2%

KEY (CORRECT ANSWERS)

1. D
2. B
3. C
4. C
5. D

6. A
7. C
8. C
9. A
10. C

11. A
12. B
13. B
14. C
15. C

16. D
17. B
18. D
19. B
20. B

21. D
22. B
23. D
24. D
25. A

TEST 4

DIRECTIONS: Each question or incomplete statement is followed by several suggested answers of completions. Select the one that best answers the question or complete the statement. *PRINT THE LETTER OF THE CORRECT ANSWER IN THE SPACE AT THE RIGHT.*

1. Imagine you are assigned a project for which you do not have the required competency and experience to manage. What is the best plan of action?
    A. Make sure that you disclose any areas of improvement that need to be immediately addressed with the project sponsor before accepting the assignment
    B. Do not inform anyone about the gaps and learn as much as you can before any critical activity is due for delivery
    C. Consider the opportunity as a stepping stone for your career development and accept it
    D. Tell your boss that you cannot manage as you do not have the relevant experience and decline it

1.___

2. You are the project manager of a new project and are involved in selecting a vendor for acquiring products required for the project. Your close friend is running a company that is also very competitive and a reputed one along with other vendors who are competing for the bid. How can you handle this situation?
    A. Do not participate in the vendor selection process as this may be considered a conflict of interest
    B. Provide information to help your friend get the contract as you are the project manager of the project
    C. Do not inform anyone about your personal contact and be involved in the vendor selection process as normal
    D. Discuss with your project sponsor the possibility of a conflict of interest and leave the decision to him on the next steps

2.___

3. You have provided good guidance to your team members and this has resulted in successful execution of all of the phases involved. There was a particular phase that has been identified as very critical and the presence of a technical expert helped achieve this success. In the senior management review meeting you were credited with the success of the project, with specific mention of that particular phase. What do you do in this situation?
    A. Accept the appreciation and feel proud about the success of the project
    B. Do not mention anything about the technical expert role as you were the project manager for this project
    C. Give credit to the technical expert and let the senior management know how the presence of the technical expert helped the team to be successful
    D. Accept the appreciation from the senior management and thank the technical expert in private for achieving this success

3.___

4. As a project manager you are preparing status reports for a meeting with the stakeholders. One of your team members has come out with an issue that will cause some delay in the project timeline. You have a plan that can be implemented to make sure that this issue can be managed without causing any delay in the timeline, but you currently do not have the time to update the project plan. How will you handle this situation?
    A. Present the status of the project as *on-track* without discussing anything about this issue as you will have time to prepare before the next meeting
    B. Cancel the meeting as you do not have the time to update the details to be provided to the stakeholders
    C. Present the status of the project *as-is* without minimizing the effect of the delay and discuss details of the planned approach to solve this issue
    D. Fire your team that is responsible for causing this delay as it has created a bad impression of you amongst the stakeholders

5. John is an Associate Director in a pharmaceutical company managing its internal projects. He has presented whitepapers on project execution methodologies and is highly respected within the organization. He also regularly conducts workshops & lectures in coordination with PMO. What kind of power does John possess?
    A. Referent power
    B. Coercive power
    C. Reward power
    D. Expert power

6. You are a project manager working for a non-profit organization. You had been assigned a project that is in the initial stage and involves development of an eco-system in a large community. You are reviewing the deliverables and templates from similar projects that are available in the company lessons learnt knowledge base. Which item will be of much importance to you?
    A. Project Information Management System
    B. Enterprise Environmental Factors
    C. Organization Process Assets
    D. Standard Templates

7. A project that you were managing is nearing completion. As part of the deliverables you are required to complete lessons-learned documentation of the project. What is the primary purpose of creating lessons-learned documentation?
    A. Provide information of project success
    B. Help identify all the failures
    C. Provide information on minimizing negative impacts and maximizing positive events for future projects of similar nature
    D. Comply with the organization's objectives

8. You are managing project teams that work from different locations and there has been issues with the teams' ability to effectively perform. This has resulted in delay in timeline. Which kind of team development technique would be most effective in this situation?
    A. Mediation
    B. Training
    C. Co-location
    D. Rewards

9. The project sponsor has requested that you create a project charter for a new project that you will manage next month. Which document will you utilize to create the project charter that will justify the need for the project?
    A. Project SOW
    B. Business Need
    C. Business Case
    D. Cost-benefit Analysis

10. An audit is being performed by a team for the project you are managing. The team reports that the standards utilized need to be analyzed as several processes that are not relevant to the current project.
What is the process that the team is currently involved?
    A. Quality planning
    B. Quality control
    C. Quality assurance
    D. Benchmark creation

11. The change control board of your organization has approved changes that were submitted and the project team is executing them.
What would this process be considered?
    A. Executing the change request
    B. Implementing a corrective action
    C. Gold-plating
    D. Approving the change request

12. Which is the primary technique that is carried out to ensure that a contract award is executed correctly or not?
    A. Litigation
    B. Contract negotiation
    C. Inspections
    D. Procurement audit

13. In the final stages of completing a project, you and your team are involved in creating the project report that will be presented to the stakeholders. Which of the following information is not appropriate to be included in the final report?
    A. Recommendations from your team
    B. Project success factors
    C. WBS dictionary
    D. Details of the process improvements

14. At the completion of a project, your team has completed the lessons-learned documentation and archived in the database. Who should have access to these documents?
    A. Project team members
    B. Operations department
    C. All of the company's members
    D. Functional managers

15. You are project manager for a large project that is in the final stages of completion and you need to formally provide information on the major milestone achieved. You are also in need of immediate feedback from the stakeholders. Which is the best communication method to meet this requirement?
    A. E-mail
    B. Web publishing
    C. Meeting
    D. Videoconferencing

16. Which document will formally authorize a project manager to start the project?
    A. Project SOW
    B. Project Charter
    C. Business Case
    D. Stakeholder Register

17. Which of the following documents would be utilized to ascertain the project's investment worthiness?
    A. Project Charter
    B. Business Case
    C. Business Need
    D. Procurement documents

18. Which of the following conflict resolution is considered as Lose-lose solution?   18._____
    A. Problem-solving   C. Compromising
    B. Forcing   D. Withdrawing

19. McGregor's Theory states that all workers fit into one of the two groups. Which of the   19._____
    following theories believes that people are willing to work on their own and need less
    supervision?
    A. Theory X   C. Maslow's Hierarchy
    B. Theory Y   D. Expectancy

20. The major cause for conflicts on a project are schedule, project priorities and _____.   20._____

    A. cost   C. personality
    B. resources   D. management

21. The project manager is responsible for   21._____
    A. the success of the project
    B. achieving the project objectives
    C. authorizing the project
    D. performing the project work

22. Which of the following actions correspond to reducing the consequences of future   22._____
    problems?
    A. Corrective action
    B. Preventive action
    C. Defect repair
    D. Change request

23. As a project manager for a large-scale project, you are in the process of procuring   23._____
    materials required for the project. Which of the following documents will you not
    be responsible for?
    A. Procurement documents
    B. Procurement statements of work
    C. Source selection criteria
    D. Proposals

24. During which process group will the detailed requirements be gathered?   24._____
    A. Initiating
    B. Planning
    C. Executing
    D. Closing

25. The values that illustrate PMIs code of ethics and professional conduct are   25._____
    A. respect, honesty, responsibility and honorability
    B. honesty, cultural diversity, integrity and responsibility
    C. fairness, responsibility, honesty and respect
    D. honorability, fairness, respect and responsibility

KEY (CORRECT ANSWERS)

1. A
2. D
3. C
4. C
5. D

6. C
7. C
8. C
9. C
10. C

11. A
12. D
13. C
14. C
15. D

16. B
17. B
18. C
19. B
20. B

21. B
22. B
23. D
24. B
25. C

EXAMINATION SECTION
TEST 1

DIRECTIONS: Each question or incomplete statement is followed by several suggested answers of completions. Select the one that BEST answers the question or Complete the statement. *PRINT THE LETTER OF THE CORRECT ANSWER IN THE SPACE AT THE RIGHT.*

1. An accepted deadline for a project approaches. However, the project manager realizes only 85% of the work has been completed. The project manager then issues a change request.
   What should the change request authorize?

   A. Corrective action based on causes
   B. Escalation approval to use contingency funding
   C. Additional resources using the contingency fund
   D. Team overtime to meet schedule

   1.____

2. _____ is a valid tool or technique to assist the project manager to assure the success of the process improvement plan.

   A. Benchmarking
   B. Change control system
   C. Process analysis
   D. Configuration management system

   2.____

3. A project manager meets with the project team to review lessons learned from previous projects. In what activity is the team involved?

   A. Performance management
   B. Project team status meeting
   C. Scope identification
   D. Risk identification

   3.____

4. _____ process helps you to purchase goods from external suppliers.

   A. Quality management
   B. Procurement management
   C. Cost management
   D. Communication management

   4.____

5. Which of the following is not involved in procurement management?

   A. Review supplier performance against contract
   B. Identify and resolve supplier performance issues
   C. Communicate the status to management
   D. Manage a WBS

   5.____

6. _____ contract is advantageous to a buyer.

   A. Fixed price
   B. Cost reimbursable
   C. Time and material
   D. Fixed price plus incentive

   6.____

7. Which of the following contracts is advantageous to a seller?

    A. Fixed price
    B. Cost reimbursable
    C. Time and material
    D. Fixed price plus incentive

8. Tom is a manager of a project whose deliverable has many uncertainties associated with it. What kind of contract should he use during the procurement process?

    A. Fixed price
    B. Cost reimbursable
    C. Time and material
    D. Fixed price plus incentive

9. Cost plus _____ is not a cost-reimbursable contract.

    A. fixed fee
    B. fee
    C. fixed time
    D. incentive fee

10. _____ type of contract helps both the seller and buyer to save, if the performance criteria are exceeded.

    A. Cost plus fixed fee
    B. Cost plus fee
    C. Cost plus fixed time
    D. Cost plus incentive fee

11. A project manager with a construction company. She has to complete a project in a specified time, but does have enough time to send the job out for bids. What type of contract would save her time?

    A. Fixed price
    B. Cost reimbursable
    C. Time and material
    D. Fixed price plus incentive

12. The major type(s) of standard warranty (ies) that are used in the business environment is (are):

    A. express
    B. negotiated
    C. implied
    D. A and C

13. During contract management, the project manager must consider the

    A. acquisition process and contract administration
    B. contract administration and ecological environment
    C. ecological environment and acquisition process
    D. offer, acceptance and consideration

14. Which contract type places the most risk on the seller?   14._____

    A. Cost plus percentage fee
    B. Cost plus incentive fee
    C. Cost plus fixed fee
    D. Firm fixed price

15. Finalizing project close-out happens when a project manager   15._____

    A. archives the project records
    B. completes the contract
    C. complete lessons learned
    D. reassigns the team

16. Unit price contract is fair to both owner and contractor,   16._____

    A. as the actual volumes will be measured and paid as the work proceeds
    B. as the owner will provide bill of quantities
    C. as both are absorbing an equal amount of risk
    D. all of the above

17. Bill is the manager of a project that requires different areas of expertise.   17._____
    Which one of the following contracts should he sign?

    A. Fixed price
    B. Cost reimbursable
    C. Time and material
    D. Unit price

18. Which of the following contracts is commonly used in projects that involve pilot   18._____
    programs or harness new technologies?

    A. Fixed price
    B. Incentive
    C. Time and material
    D. Unit price

19. Procurement cycle involves all of the following steps EXCEPT   19._____

    A. supplier contract
    B. renewal
    C. sending a proposal
    D. information gathering

20. What would happen if a project manager does not take up a background review during the   20._____
    procurement process?

    A. Price might not be negotiated
    B. Credibility of the goods might not be validated
    C. Goods might not be shipped
    D. Both A and B

21. _____ is not a part of a procurement document.

    A. Buyer's commencement to the bid
    B. Summons by the financially responsible party
    C. Establishing terms and conditions of a contract
    D. Roles of responsibilities of internal team

22. Which of the following is NOT an example of a procurement document?

    A. Offers
    B. Contracts
    C. Project record archives
    D. Request for quotation

23. A project manager needs to follow _____ for a good procurement document to be drafted.

    A. clear definition of the responsibilities, rights and commitments of both parties in the contract
    B. clear definition of the nature and quality of the goods or services to be provided
    C. clear and easy to understand language
    D. all of the above

24. Which of the following is not a concern with respect to procurement management?

    A. Reassigning the team
    B. Not all goods and services that a business requires need to be purchased from outside
    C. You would need to have a good idea of what you exactly require and then go on to consider various options and alternatives
    D. You would need to consider different criteria, apart from just the cost, to finally decide on which supplier you would want to go with.

25. Source qualifications are a part of the _____ phase of Acquisition Process Cycle.

    A. post-award
    B. pre-award
    C. award
    D. origination

KEY (CORRECT ANSWERS)

1. A
2. C
3. D
4. B
5. D

6. A
7. B
8. B
9. C
10. D

11. C
12. D
13. A
14. D
15. B

16. C
17. D
18. B
19. C
20. B

21. D
22. C
23. D
24. A
25. C

TEST 2

DIRECTIONS: Each question or incomplete statement is followed by several suggested answers of completions. Select the one that BEST answers the question or Complete the statement. *PRINT THE LETTER OF THE CORRECT ANSWER IN THE SPACE AT THE RIGHT.*

1. Which of the following project tools details the project scope?　　　　1._____

    A. Project plan
    B. Gantt chart
    C. Milestone checklist
    D. Score cards

2. Which of the following is NOT a project tool?　　　　2._____

    A. Gantt chart
    B. Milestone checklist
    C. Score cards
    D. MS project

3. _____ is accompanied by project audits by a third party. As a result, non-compliance and action items are tracked.　　　　3._____

    A. Gantt chart
    B. Milestone checklist
    C. Project reviews
    D. Delivery reviews

4. An IT project manager, is involved in tracking his team's performance. Which tool would he use to gauge this performance?　　　　4._____

    A. Score cards
    B. Gantt chart
    C. Project management software
    D. Milestone checklist

5. What tool does a manager use to track the interdependencies of each project activity?　　　　5._____

    A. Project plan
    B. Gantt chart
    C. Project management software
    D. Milestone checklist

6. Which tool would be used for a manager to determine if he or she is on track in terms of project progress?　　　　6._____

    A. Project management software
    B. Delivery reviews
    C. Project reviews
    D. Milestone checklist

7. Which of the following tools is used for individual member promotion?

    A. Delivery reviews
    B. Score cards
    C. Project reviews
    D. Milestone checklist

8. Which of the following is NOT a project management process?

    A. Project planning
    B. Project initiation
    C. Project management software
    D. Closeout and evaluation

9. _____ is the phase in which the service provider proves the eligibility and ability of completing the project to the client.

    A. Pre-sale period
    B. Project execution
    C. Sign-off
    D. Closeout and evaluation

10. Controlling of the project could be done by following all of the following protocols EXCEPT

    A. communication plan
    B. quality assurance test plan
    C. test plan
    D. project plan

11. A manager wants his project to be successful and hence verifies the successful outcome of every activity leading to successful completion of the project. Which of the following activities would he use to do so?

    A. Control
    B. Test plan
    C. Project plan
    D. Validation

12. What happens during the closeout and evaluation phase?

    A. Evaluation of the entire project
    B. Hand over the implemented system
    C. Identifying mistakes and taking necessary action
    D. All of the above

13. A project manager, is conducting validation and verification functions. Which team's assistance would she need in order to do so?

    A. Quality assurance team
    B. Project team
    C. Client team
    D. Third-party vendor

14. Tracking the effort and cost of the project is done during _____.

    A. project execution
    B. control and validation
    C. closeout and evaluation
    D. communication plan

15. _____ is the entity created for governing the processes, practices, tools and other activities related to project management in an organization.

    A. Project management office
    B. Project management software
    C. Quality assurance
    D. None of the above

16. A project management office must be built with the following considerations EXCEPT

    A. process optimization
    B. productivity enhancement
    C. building the bottom line of their organization
    D. none of the above

17. An advantage of a project management office is that it

    A. helps cut down staff
    B. helps cut down resources
    C. refines the processes related to project management
    D. all of the above

18. A project management office could fail because of

    A. lack of executive management support
    B. incapability
    C. it adds figures to the bottom line of the company
    D. both A and B

19. _____ is used to analyze the difficulties that may arise due to the execution of the project.

    A. Project management office
    B. Project management triangle
    C. Both A and B
    D. None of the above

20. The three constraints in a project management triangle are _____.

    A. time, cost and scope
    B. time, resources and quality
    C. time, resources and people
    D. time, resources and cost

21. A project manager, is experiencing challenges related to project triangle and hence finds difficulty in achieving the project objectives. Which of the following skills would help her?   21._____

    A. Time management
    B. Effective communication
    C. Managing people
    D. All of the above

22. _____ is NOT a role of a project manager.   22._____

    A. Carrying out basic project tasks
    B. Keeping stakeholders informed on the project progress
    C. Defining project scope and assigning tasks to team members
    D. Setting objectives

23. Kathy is advising Nicole on the goals and challenges a project manager must consider. Which of the following should she discuss?   23._____

    A. Deadlines
    B. Client satisfaction
    C. No budget overrun
    D. All of the above

24. Team management deals with all of the following EXCEPT   24._____

    A. providing incentives and encouragement
    B. maintaining warm and friendly relationship with teammates
    C. meeting requirements of the client
    D. including them in project related decisions

25. _____ is vital to win client satisfaction.   25._____

    A. Finishing the work on scheduled time
    B. Ensuring that most standards are met
    C. Having a limited relationship with the client
    D. All of the above

KEY (CORRECT ANSWERS)

1. A
2. D
3. C
4. A
5. B

6. D
7. B
8. C
9. A
10. C

11. D
12. D
13. A
14. A
15. A

16. D
17. C
18. D
19. B
20. A

21. D
22. A
23. D
24. C
25. A

TEST 3

DIRECTIONS: Each question or incomplete statement is followed by several suggested answers of completions. Select the one that BEST answers the question or Complete the statement. *PRINT THE LETTER OF THE CORRECT ANSWER IN THE SPACE AT THE RIGHT.*

1. What type of strategy is followed by a manager before his workforce focuses on with performance?

    A. Activators
    B. Behaviors
    C. Consequences
    D. Deviators

2. _____ define how the workforce performs or behaves within the activity or situation as a result of activators or consequences.

    A. Deviators
    B. Consequences
    C. Behaviors
    D. Activators

3. _____ explain how the manager handles the workforce after the performance.

    A. Deviators
    B. Consequences
    C. Behaviors
    D. Activators

4. Which of the following is found to have a great impact on workforce behavior?

    A. Deviators
    B. Consequences
    C. Behaviors
    D. Activators

5. Nancy, an IT project manager, is keen to delegate her work. She is aware that a good manager's role is about delegating work effectively in order to complete the task. What should she consider before delegating?

    A. Delegating the work with clear instructions and expectations stated
    B. Providing enough moral support
    C. Identify individuals that are capable of carrying out a particular task
    D. All the above

6. Which of the following is NOT a tool related to controlling and assuring quality?

    A. Check sheet
    B. Cause-and-effect diagram
    C. Activators
    D. Scatter diagram

7. _____ are used for understanding business, implementation and organizational problems.

    A. Cause-and-effect diagrams
    B. Scatter diagrams
    C. Control charts
    D. Pareto charts

8. Jim is replacing the earlier project manager in the middle of the project and hard-pressed with time. He has to work on a priority basis.
   Which of the following tools would he use to identify priorities?

   A. Cause-and-effect diagram
   B. Scatter diagram
   C. Control chart
   D. Pareto chart

Questions 9-11 refer to the following chart.

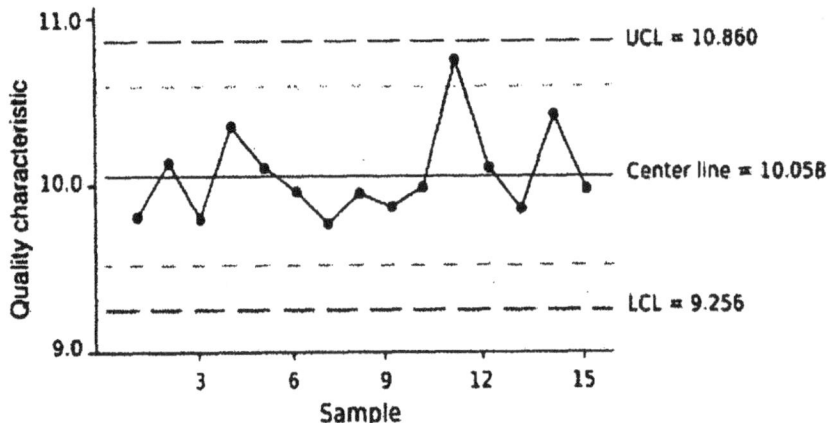

9. What type of tool is this?

   A. Control chart
   B. Flow chart
   C. Scatter diagram
   D. Pareto chart

10. The above-mentioned chart/tool is used for _____.

    A. identifying sets of priorities
    B. comparing two variables
    C. monitoring the performance of a process
    D. gathering and organizing data

11. The above chart/tool could be used to identify all of the following EXCEPT

    A. the stability of the process
    B. the common cause of variation
    C. the parameter(s) that have the highest impact on the specific concern
    D. conditions where the monitoring team needs to react

12. Which of the following tools would a project manager use to perform a trend analysis?

    A. Flow chart
    B. Scatter diagram
    C. Cause-and-effect diagram
    D. Pareto chart

13. _____ is/are a common and simple method used by project managers to arrive at an effective cause-and-effect diagram.

    A. Survey
    B. Brainstorming
    C. Informal discussions
    D. Formal presentations

14. Which of the following tools should a project manager use to gain a brief understanding of the project's critical path?

    A. Flow chart
    B. Pareto chart
    C. Histogram
    D. Check sheet

15. _____ is NOT a step involved in the benchmarking process.

    A. Planning
    B. Analysis of data
    C. Monitoring
    D. None of the above

16. As a project manager, where will you collect primary data when you collect information?

    i) Benchmarked company
    ii) Press
    iii) Publication
    iv) Website

    A. Only I
    B. Both I and II
    C. I, II, III and IV
    D. Both I and IV

17. Which of the following methods is recommended to conduct primary research?

    A. E-mail
    B. Referring to the website of other companies
    C. Telephone
    D. Face-to-face interviews

18. Analysis of data involves all of the following EXCEPT

    A. sharing data with all the stakeholders
    B. data presentation
    C. results projection
    D. classifying the performance gaps in processes

19. _____ is referred to as an enabler, which will help project managers to act wisely.

   A. Projection of results
   B. Performance gap identification
   C. Root cause of performance gaps
   D. Presentation of data

20. Which of the following needs to be done in order to monitor the quality of the project?

   A. Evaluating the progress made
   B. Reiterating the impact of change
   C. Making necessary adjustments
   D. All the above

Use the following cause-and-effect diagram to answer questions 21 through 23.

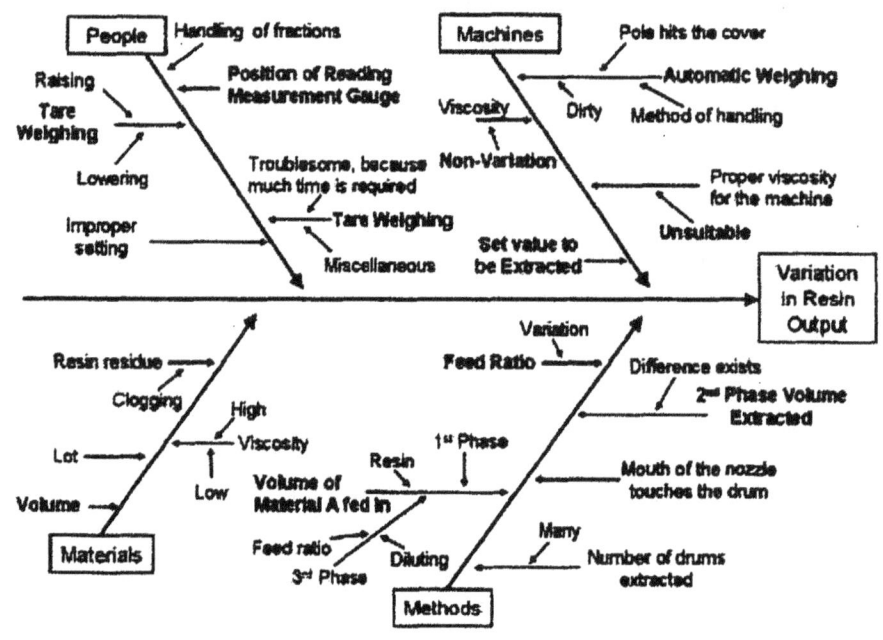

21. Which of the following is NOT represented in this diagram?

   A. Problem
   B. Major cause of the problem
   C. Contributing factors
   D. Possible causes of the problem

22. What is the effect with respect to the diagram?

   A. Materials
   B. Methods
   C. Variation in Resin Output
   D. People

23. As a project manager, what will you do to gain a better understanding of the problems and handling them? 23.____

    A. Investigations
    B. Surveys
    C. Interviews
    D. All the above

24. Kotter's change management process involves all the following steps EXCEPT 24.____

    A. building a team
    B. resource management
    C. creating a vision
    D. removing obstacles

25. _____ lets team members know why they are working on a change initiative. 25.____

    A. Removing obstacles
    B. Building a team
    C. Integrating the change
    D. Creating a vision

KEY (CORRECT ANSWERS)

1. A
2. C
3. B
4. B
5. D

6. C
7. A
8. D
9. A
10. C

11. C
12. B
13. B
14. A
15. D

16. C
17. B
18. A
19. C
20. D

21. B
22. C
23. D
24. B
25. D

TEST 4

DIRECTIONS: Each question or incomplete statement is followed by several suggested answers of completions. Select the one that best answers the question or Complete the statement. *PRINT THE LETTER OF THE CORRECT ANSWER IN THE SPACE AT THE RIGHT.*

1. Which of the following is NOT a communication blocker?   1.____
   A. Judging
   B. Accusing
   C. Globalizing
   D. Listening

2. Using words like "always" and "never" is an example of _____.   2.____
   A. judging
   B. accusing
   C. globalizing
   D. listening

3. What should you do as a project manager to eliminate communication blockers?   3.____
   A. Encourage others to avoid communication blockers by educating them
   B. Be aware of the various blockers and take steps to remove them
   C. Model to promote effective and empathetic communication
   D. All of the above

4. What would happen if there were no proper communication channel?   4.____
   A. Inefficient flow of information
   B. Clarity among employees on what is expected of them
   C. Sense of company mind/common vision among employees
   D. Clarity among employees on the happening within the company

5. As a project manager, you could use any one of the following types of language EXCEPT _____ for communicating with your team.   5.____
   A. formal
   B. insulting
   C. informal
   D. unofficial

6. A(n) _____ is/are NOT an example of formal communication.   6.____
   A. annual report
   B. business plan
   C. social gathering
   D. review meetings

7. _____ types of communication are used to communicate company policies, goals and procedures.
    A. Formal
    B. Informal
    C. Unofficial
    D. None of the above

7._____

8. _____ is NOT an example of informal communication.
    A. Survey
    B. Quality circle
    C. Team work
    D. Training program

8._____

9. "Grapevine" is an example of _____ communication.
    A. Formal
    B. Informal
    C. Unofficial
    D. None of the above

9._____

10. What question would you NOT consider as a project manager before choosing the right method to communicate?
    A. Who is the target audience?
    B. Will it lead to employee productivity?
    C. What kind of information would be helpful for clarity among employees?
    D. Which is the best way to threaten the employees?

10._____

11. Which of the following is not included in "The Five Ws of Communication Management"?
    A. What information would prompt employees to work out of fear?
    B. What information is essential for the project?
    C. What is the time required for the communication to happen effectively?
    D. Who requires information and what type of information is required?

11._____

12. _____ refers to developing a message.
    A. Decoding
    B. Encoding
    C. Transmission
    D. Feedback

12._____

13. _____ refers to interpreting the message.
    A. Decoding
    B. Encoding
    C. Transmission
    D. Feedback

14. Which of the following is not necessarily involved in a communication process?
    A. Sender
    B. Transmission
    C. Vision
    D. Receiver

15. _____ is NOT a sign of active listening.
    A. Making eye contact
    B. Asking questions to gain clarity
    C. Using gestures like nodding head
    D. Using gestures that distract the speaker

16. Madeline is a project manager and involved in conflict management. Which of the following should she use to manage a conflict?
    A. Identify actions that resolve conflicts
    B. Identify actions that would aggravate conflicts
    C. Consider different methods of resolving the conflict
    D. All the above

17. A managerial action that would NOT aggravate conflict is _____.
    A. poor communication
    B. assertive style of leadership
    C. ill-defined expectations
    D. authoritative style of leadership

18. An example of a managerial action that would NOT minimize a conflict is
    A. well-defined job descriptions
    B. participative approach
    C. submissive style of leadership
    D. fostering team spirit

19. Which of the following methods could you use as a project manager to handle conflicts?
    A. Flight
    B. Fake
    C. Fight
    D. All of the above

20. _____ is the term used when people run away from problems instead of confronting them and turn to avoidance as a means of handling conflict.
    A. Flight
    B. Fake
    C. Fight
    D. Fold

21. _____ is the term used when an individual is made to agree to a solution by means of browbeating.
    A. Flight
    B. Fake
    C. Fight
    D. Fold

22. Which of the following is NOT a step in conflict management?
    A. Choose the best solution that satisfy most people most of the time and implement this
    B. Engage in participatory dialogue and find a range of solutions that will be acceptable to all the parties concerned
    C. Eliminate those who promote mutual understanding and acceptance
    D. Identify the limiting resource or constraint that is generally at the root cause of the conflict

23. Which of the following is NOT a skill required for conflict resolution?
    A. Clarity in communication
    B. Aggressiveness
    C. Negotiation
    D. Listening

24. _____ is essential to be prepared for any problems that may arise when it is least expected.
    A. Conflict management
    B. Communication management
    C. Crisis management
    D. None of the above

25. Which of the following is NOT a type of crisis?
    A. Financial
    B. Technological
    C. Natural
    D. Negotiation

25._____

KEY (CORRECT ANSWERS)

1. D
2. C
3. D
4. A
5. B

6. C
7. A
8. A
9. C
10. D

11. A
12. B
13. A
14. C
15. D

16. D
17. B
18. C
19. D
20. A

21. D
22. C
23. B
24. C
25. D

EXAMINATION SECTION
TEST 1

DIRECTIONS: Each question or incomplete statement is followed by several suggested answers or completions. Select the one that BEST answers the question or completes the statement. *PRINT THE LETTER OF THE CORRECT ANSWER IN THE SPACE AT THE RIGHT.*

1. When conducting a needs assessment for the purpose of education planning, an agency's FIRST step is to identify or provide
    A. a profile of population characteristics
    B. barriers to participation
    C. existing resources
    D. profiles of competing resources

    1.____

2. Research has demonstrated that of the following, the MOST effective medium for communicating with external publics is(are)
    A. video news releases   B. television
    C. radio   D. newspapers

    2.____

3. Basic ideas behind the effort to influence the attitudes and behaviors of a constituency include each of the following EXCEPT the idea that
    A. words, rather than actions or events, are most likely to motivate
    B. demands for action are a usual response
    C. self-interest usually figures heavily into public involvement
    D. the reliability of change programs is difficult to assess

    3.____

4. An agency representative is trying to craft a pithy message to constituents in order to encourage the use of agency program resources.
    Choosing an audience for such messages is easiest when the message
    A. is project- or behavior-based   B. is combined with other messages
    C. is abstract   D. has a broad appeal

    4.____

5. Of the following factors, the MOST important to the success of an agency's external education or communication programs is the
    A. amount of resources used to implement them
    B. public's prior experiences with the agency
    C. real value of the program to the public
    D. commitment of the internal audience

    5.____

6. A representative for a state agency is being interviewed by a reporter from a local news network. The representative is being asked to defend a program that is extremely unpopular in certain parts of the municipality.
    When a constituency is known to be opposed to a position, the MOST useful communication strategy is to present

    6.____

A. only the arguments that are consistent with constituents' views
B. only the agency's side of the issue
C. both sides of the argument as clearly as possible
D. both sides of the argument, omitting key information about the opposing position

7. The MOST significant barriers to effective agency community relations include
   I. widespread distrust of communication strategies
   II. the media's "watchdog" stance
   III. public apathy
   IV. statutory opposition

   The CORRECT answer is:
   A. I only   B. I and II   C. II and III   D. III and IV

8. In conducting an education program, many agencies use workshops and seminars in a classroom setting.
   Advantages of classroom-style teaching over other means of educating the public include each of the following, EXCEPT
   A. enabling an instructor to verify learning through testing and interaction with the target audience
   B. enabling hands-on practice and other participatory learning techniques
   C. ability to reach an unlimited number of participants in a given length of time
   D. ability to convey the latest, most up-to-date information

9. The _____ model of community relations is characterized by an attempt to persuade the public to adopt the agency's point of view.
   A. two-way symmetric   B. two-way asymmetric
   C. public information   D. press agency/publicity

10. Important elements of an internal situation analysis include the
    I. list of agency opponents   II. communication audit
    III. updated organizational almanac IV. stakeholder analysis

    The CORRECT answer is:
    A. I and II   B. I, II, and III   C. II and III   D. I, II, III and IV

11. Government agency information efforts typically involve each of the following objectives, EXCEPT to
    A. implement changes in the policies of government agencies to align with public opinion
    B. communicate the work of agencies
    C. explain agency techniques in a way that invites input from citizens
    D. provide citizen feedback to government administrators

12. Factors that are likely to influence the effectiveness of an educational campaign include the
    I. level of homogeneity among intended participants
    II. number and types of media used
    III. receptivity of the intended participants
    IV. level of specificity in the message or behavior to be taught

    The CORRECT answer is:
    A. I and II   B. I, II, and III   C. II and III   D. I, II, III, and IV

13. An agency representative is writing instructional objectives that will later help to measure the effectiveness of an educational program.
    Which of the following verbs, included in an objective, would be MOST helpful for the purpose of measuring effectiveness?
    A. Know   B. Identify   C. Learn   D. Comprehend

14. A state education agency wants to encourage participation in a program that has just received a boost through new federal legislation. The program is intended to include participants from a wide variety of socioeconomic and other demographic characteristics. The agency wants to launch a broad-based program that will inform virtually every interested party in the state about the program's new circumstances.
    In attempting to deliver this message to such a wide-ranging constituency, the agency's BEST practice would be to
    A. broadcast the same message through as many different media channels as possible
    B. focus on one discrete segment of the public at a time
    C. craft a message whose appeal is as broad as the public itself
    D. let the program's achievements speak for themselves and rely on word-of-mouth

15. Advantages associated with using the World Wide Web as an educational tool include
    I. an appeal to younger generations of the public
    II. visually-oriented, interactive learning
    III. learning that is not confined by space, time, or institutional association
    IV. a variety of methods for verifying use and learning

    The CORRECT answer is:
    A. I only   B. I and II   C. I, II, and III   D. I, II, II, and IV

16. In agencies involved in health care, community relations is a critical function because it
    A. serves as an intermediary between the agency and consumers
    B. generates a clear mission statement for agency goals and priorities
    C. ensures patient privacy while satisfying the media's right to information
    D. helps marketing professionals determine the wants and needs of agency constituents

17. After an extensive campaign to promote its newest program to constituents, an agency learns that most of the audience did not understand the intended message.
MOST likely, the agency has
   A. chosen words that were intended to inform, rather than persuade
   B. not accurately interpreted what the audience really needed to know
   C. overestimated the ability of the audience to receive and process the message
   D. compensated for noise that may have interrupted the message

17.____

18. The necessary elements that lead to conviction and motivation in the minds of participants in an educational or information program include each of the following, EXCEPT the _____ of the message.
   A. acceptability   B. intensity
   C. single-channel appeal D. pervasiveness

18.____

19. Printed materials are often at the core of educational programs provided by public agencies.
The PRIMARY disadvantage associated with print is that it
   A. does not enable comprehensive treatment of a topic
   B. is generally unreliable in term of assessing results
   C. is often the most expensive medium available
   D. is constrained by time

19.____

20. Traditional thinking on public opinion holds that there is about _____ percent of the public who are pivotal to shifting the balance and momentum of opinion—they are concerned about an issue, but not fanatical, and interested enough to pay attention to a reasoned discussion.
   A. 2   B. 10   C. 33   D. 51

20.____

21. One of the most useful guidelines for influencing attitude change among people is to
   A. invite the target audience to come to you, rather than approaching them
   B. use moral appeals as the primary approach
   C. use concrete images to enable people to see the results of behaviors or indifference
   D. offer tangible rewards to people for changes in behavior

21.____

22. An agency is attempting to evaluate the effectiveness of its educational program. For this purpose, it wants to observe several focus groups discussing the same program.
Which of the following would NOT be a guideline for the use of focus groups?
   A. Focus groups should only include those who have participated in the program.
   B. Be sure to accurately record the discussion.
   C. The same questions should be asked at each focus group meeting.
   D. It is often helpful to have a neutral, non-agency employee facilitate discussions.

22.____

23. Research consistently shows that _____ is the determinant most likely to make a newspaper editor run a news release.
    A. novelty   B. prominence   C. proximity   D. conflict

24. Which of the following is NOT one of the major variables to take into account when considering a population-needs assessment?
    A. State of program development   B. Resources available
    C. Demographics   D. Community attitudes

25. The FIRST step in any communications audit is to
    A. develop a research instrument
    B. determine how the organization currently communicates
    C. hire a contractor
    D. determine which audience to assess

KEY (CORRECT ANSWERS)

1.	A	11.	A
2.	D	12.	D
3.	A	13.	B
4.	A	14.	B
5.	D	15.	C
6.	C	16.	A
7.	D	17.	B
8.	C	18.	C
9.	B	19.	B
10.	C	20.	B

21.	C
22.	A
23.	C
24.	C
25.	D

TEST 2

DIRECTIONS: Each question or incomplete statement is followed by several suggested answers or completions. Select the one that BEST answers the question or completes the statement. *PRINT THE LETTER OF THE CORRECT ANSWER IN THE SPACE AT THE RIGHT.*

1. A public relations practitioner at an agency has just composed a press release highlighting a program's recent accomplishments and success stories.
   In pitching such releases to print outlets, the practitioner should
   I. e-mail, mail, or send them by messenger
   II. address them to "editor" or "news director"
   III. have an assistant call all media contacts by telephone
   IV. ask reporters or editors how they prefer to receive them

   The CORRECT answer is:
   A. I and II   B. I and IV   C. II, III, and IV   D. III only

   1._____

2. The "output goals" of an educational program are MOST likely to include
   A. specified ratings of services by participants on a standardized scale
   B. observable effects on a given community or clientele
   C. the number of instructional hours provided
   D. the number of participants served

   2._____

3. An agency wants to evaluate satisfaction levels among program participants, and mails out questionnaires to everyone who has been enrolled in the last year.
   The PRIMARY problem associated with this method of evaluative research is that it
   A. poses a significant inconvenience for respondents
   B. is inordinately expensive
   C. does not allow for follow-up or clarification questions
   D. usually involves a low response rate

   3._____

4. A communications audit is an important tool for measuring
   A. the depth of penetration of a particular message or program
   B. the cost of the organization's information campaigns
   C. how key audiences perceive an organization
   D. the commitment of internal stakeholders

   4._____

5. The "ABCs" of written learning objectives include each of the following, EXCEPT
   A. Audience   B. Behavior   C. Conditions   D. Delineation

   5._____

6. When attempting to change the behaviors of constituents, it is important to keep in mind that
   I. most people are skeptical of communications that try to get them to change their behaviors
   II. in most cases, a person selects the media to which he exposes himself
   III. people tend to react defensively to messages or programs that rely on fear as a motivating factor
   IV. programs should aim for the broadest appeal possible in order to include as many participants as possible

   The CORRECT answer is:
   A. I and II   B. I, II and III   C. II and III   D. I, II, III, and IV

7. The "laws" of public opinion include the idea that it is
   A. useful for anticipating emergencies
   B. not sensitive to important events
   C. basically determined by self-interest
   D. sustainable through persistent appeals

8. Which of the following types of evaluations is used to measure public attitudes before and after an information/educational program?
   A. Retrieval study
   B. Copy test
   C. Quota sampling
   D. Benchmark study

9. The PRIMARY source for internal communications is(are) usually
   A. flow charts
   B. meetings
   C. voice mail
   D. printed publications

10. An agency representative is putting together informational materials—brochures and a newsletter—outlining changes in one of the state's biggest benefits programs.
    In assembling print materials as a medium for delivering information to the public, the representative should keep in mind each of the following trends:
    I. For various reasons, the reading capabilities of the public are in general decline
    II. Without tables and graphs to help illustrate the changes, it is unlikely that the message will be delivered effectively
    III. Professionals and career-oriented people are highly receptive to information written in the form of a journal article or empirical study
    IV. People tend to be put off by print materials that use itemized and bulleted (●) lists

    The CORRECT answer is:
    A. I and II   B. I, II and III   C. II and III   D. I, II, III, and IV

11. Which of the following steps in a problem-oriented information campaign would typically be implemented FIRST?
    A. Deciding on tactics
    B. Determining a communications strategy
    C. Evaluating the problem's impact
    D. Developing an organizational strategy

12. A common pitfall in conducting an educational program is to
    A. aim it at the wrong target audience
    B. overfund it
    C. leave it in the hands of people who are in the business of education, rather than those with expertise in the business of the organization
    D. ignore the possibility that some other organization is meeting the same educational need for the target audience

13. The key factors that affect the credibility of an agency's educational program include
    A. organization
    B. scope
    C. sophistication
    D. penetration

14. Research on public opinion consistently demonstrates that it is
    A. easy to move people toward a strong opinion on anything, as long as they are approached directly through their emotions
    B. easier to move people away from an opinion they currently hold than to have them form an opinion about something they have not previously cared about
    C. easy to move people toward a strong opinion on anything, as long as the message appeals to their reason and intellect
    D. difficult to move people toward a strong opinion on anything, no matter what the approach

15. In conducting an education program, many agencies use meetings and conferences to educate an audience about the organization and its programs. Advantages associated with this approach include
    I. a captive audience that is known to be interested in the topic
    II. ample opportunities for verifying learning
    III. cost-efficient meeting space
    IV. the ability to provide information on a wider variety of subjects

    The CORRECT answer is:
    A. I and II   B. I, III and IV   C. II and III   D. I, II, III and IV

16. An agency is attempting to evaluate the effectiveness of its educational programs. For this purpose, it wants to observe several focus groups discussing particular programs.
    For this purpose, a focus group should never number more than _____ participants.
    A. 5   B. 10   C. 15   D. 20

17. A _____ speech is written so that several agency members can deliver it to different audiences with only minor variations.
    A. basic   B. printed   C. quota   D. pattern

18. Which of the following statements about public opinion is generally considered to be FALSE?
    A. Opinion is primarily reactive rather than proactive.
    B. People have more opinions about goals than about the means by which to achieve them.
    C. Facts tend to shift opinion in the accepted direction when opinion is not solidly structured.
    D. Public opinion is based more on information than desire.

19. An agency is trying to promote its educational program.
    As a general rule, the agency should NOT assume that
    A. people will only participate if they perceive an individual benefit
    B. promotions need to be aimed at small, discrete groups
    C. if the program is good, the audience will find out about it
    D. a variety of methods, including advertising, special events, and direct mail, should be considered

20. In planning a successful educational program, probably the first and most important question for an agency to ask is:
    A. What will be the content of the program?
    B. Who will be served by the program?
    C. When is the best time to schedule the program?
    D. Why is the program necessary?

21. Media kits are LEAST likely to contain
    A. fact sheets   B. memoranda
    C. photographs with captions   D. news releases

22. The use of pamphlets and booklets as media for communication with the public often involves the disadvantage that
    A. the messages contained within them are frequently nonspecific
    B. it is difficult to measure their effectiveness in delivering the message
    C. there are few opportunities for people to refer to them
    D. color reproduction is poor

23. The MOST important prerequisite of a good educational program is an
    A. abundance of resources to implement it
    B. individual staff unit formed for the purpose of program delivery
    C. accurate needs assessment
    D. uneducated constituency

24. After an education program has been delivered, an agency conducts a program evaluation to determine whether its objectives have been met.
General rules about how to conduct such an education program valuation include each of the following, EXCEPT that it
   A. must be done immediately after the program has been implemented
   B. should be simple and easy to use
   C. should be designed so that tabulation of responses can take place quickly and inexpensively
   D. should solicit mostly subjective, open-ended responses if the audience was large

25. Using electronic media such as television as means of educating the public is typically recommended ONLY for agencies that
   I. have a fairly simple message to begin with
   II. want to reach the masses, rather than a targeted audience
   III. have substantial financial resources
   IV. accept that they will not be able to measure the results of the campaign with much precision

   The CORRECT answer is:
   A. I and II B. I, II and III C. II and IV D. I, II, III and IV

KEY (CORRECT ANSWERS)

1. B
2. C
3. D
4. C
5. D

6. B
7. C
8. D
9. D
10. A

11. C
12. D
13. A
14. D
15. B

16. B
17. D
18. D
19. C
20. D

21. B
22. B
23. C
24. D
25. D

EXAMINATION SECTION
TEST 1

DIRECTIONS: Each question or incomplete statement is followed by several suggested answers or completions. Select the one that BEST answers the question or completes the statement. *PRINT THE LETTER OF THE CORRECT ANSWER IN THE SPACE AT THE RIGHT.*

1. A management approach widely used today is based on the belief that decisions should be made and actions should be taken by managers closest to the organization's problems.
   This style of management is MOST appropriately called _____ management.
   A. scientific
   B. means-end
   C. decentralized
   D. internal process

   1._____

2. As contrasted with tall organization structures with narrow spans of control, flat organization structures with wide spans of control MOST usually provide
   A. fast communication and information flows
   B. more levels in the organizational hierarchy
   C. fewer workers reporting to supervisors
   D. lower motivation because of tighter control standards

   2._____

3. Use of the systems approach is MOST likely to lead to
   A. consideration of the impact on the whole organization of actions taken in any part of that organization
   B. the placing of restrictions on departmental activity
   C. use of mathematical models to suboptimize production
   D. consideration of the activities of each unit of an organization as a totality without regard to the remainder of the organization

   3._____

4. An administrator, with overall responsibility for all administrative operations in a large operating agency, is considering organizing the agency's personnel office around either of the following two alternative concepts:
   Alternative I: A corps of specialists for each branch of personnel subject matter, whose skills, counsel, or work products are coordinated only by the agency personnel officer
   Alternative II: A crew of so-called *personnel generalists*, who individually work with particular segments of the organization but deal with all subspecialties of the personnel function
   The one of the following which MOST tends to be a DRAWBACK of Alternative I, as compared with Alternative II, is that
   A. training and employee relations work call for education, interests, and talents that differ from those required for classification and compensation work
   B. personnel office staff may develop only superficial familiarity with the specialized areas to which they have been assigned

   4._____

C. supervisors may fail to get continuing overall personnel advice on an integrated basis
D. the personnel specialists are likely to become so interested in and identified with the operating view as to particular cases that they lose their professional objectivity and become merely advocates of what some supervisor wants

5. The matrix summary or decision matrix is a useful tool for making choices. Its effectiveness is MOST dependent upon the user's ability to
   A. write a computer program (Fortran or Cobol)
   B. assign weights representing the relative importance of the objectives
   C. solve a set of two equations with two unknowns
   D. work with matrix algebra

6. An organizational form which is set up only on an *ad hoc* basis to meet specific goals is said PRIMARILY to use
   A. clean break departmentation
   B. matrix or task force organization
   C. scalar specialization
   D. geographic or area-wide decentralization

7. The concept of job enlargement would LEAST properly be implemented by
   A. permitting workers to follow through on tasks or projects from start to finish
   B. delegating the maximum authority possible for decision-making to lower levels in the hierarchy
   C. maximizing the number of professional classes in the classification plan
   D. training employees to grow beyond whatever tasks they have been performing

8. As used in the area of admission, the principle of *unity of command* MOST specifically means that
   A. an individual should report to only one superior for any single activity
   B. individuals make better decisions than do committees
   C. in large organizations, chains of command are normally too long
   D. an individual should not supervise over five subordinates

9. The method of operations research, statistical decision-making, and linear programming have been referred to as the tool kit of the manager.
   Utilization of these tools is LEAST useful in the performance of which of the following functions?
   A. Elimination of the need for using judgment when making decisions
   B. Facilitation of decision-making without the need for sub-optimization
   C. Quantifying problems for management study
   D. Research and analysis of management operations

10. When acting in their respective managerial capacities, the chief executive officer and the office supervisor both perform the fundamental functions of management.
    Of the following differences between the two, the one which is generally considered to be the LEAST significant is the
    A. breadth of the objectives
    B. complexity of measuring actual efficiency of performance
    C. number of decisions made
    D. organizational relationships affected by actions taken

10.____

11. The ability of operations researchers to solve complicated problems rests on their use of models.
    These models can BEST be described as
    A. mathematical statements of the problem
    B. physical constructs that simulate a work layout
    C. toy-like representations of employees in work environments
    D. role-playing simulations

11.____

12. Of the following, it is MOST likely to be proper for the agency head to allow the agency personnel officer to make final selection of appointees from certified eligible lists where there are
    A. *small* numbers of employees to be hired in newly-developed professional fields
    B. *large* numbers of persons to be hired for key managerial positions
    C. *large* numbers of persons to be hired in very routine occupations where the individual discretion of operating officials is not vital
    D. *small* numbers of persons to be hired in highly specialized professional occupations which are vital to the agency's operations

12.____

13. Of the following, an operating agency personnel office is LEAST likely to be able to exert strong influence or control within the operating agency by
    A. interpreting to the operating agency head what is intended by the directives and rules emanating from the central personnel agency
    B. establishing the key objectives of those line divisions of the operating agency employing large numbers of staff and operating under the management-by-objectives approach
    C. formulating and proposing to the agency head the internal policies and procedures on personnel matters required within the operating agency
    D. exercising certain discretionary authority in the application of the agency head's general personnel policies to actual specific situations

13.____

14. PERT is a recently developed system used PRIMARILY to
    A. evaluate the quality of applicants' background
    B. analyze and control the timing aspects of a major project
    C. control the total expenditure of agency funds within a monthly or quarterly time period
    D. analyze and control the differential effect on costs of purchasing different quantities

14.____

15. Assume that an operating agency has among its vacant positions two positions, each of which encompasses mixed duties. Both require appointees to have considerable education and experience, but these requirements are essential only for the more difficult duties of these positions. In the place of these positions, an administrator creates two new positions, one in which the higher duties are concentrated and the other with the lesser functions requiring only minimum preparation.
Of the following, it is generally MOST appropriate to characterize the administrator's action as a(n)
    A. *undesirable* example of deliberate downgrading of standards and requirements
    B. *undesirable* manipulation of the classification system for non-merit purposes
    C. *desirable* broadening of the definition of a class of positions
    D. *desirable* example of job redesign

16. Of the following, the LEAST important stumbling block to the development of personnel mobility among governmental jurisdictions is the
    A. limitations on lateral entry above junior levels in many jurisdictions
    B. continued collection of filing fees for civil service tests by many governmental jurisdictions
    C. absence of reciprocal exchange of retirement benefit eligibility between governments
    D. disparities in salary scales between governments

17. Of the following, the MAJOR disadvantage of a personnel system that features the *selection out* (forced retirement) of those who have been passed over a number of times for promotion is that such a system
    A. wastes manpower which is perfectly competent at one level but unable to rise above that level
    B. wastes funds by requiring review boards
    C. leads to excessive recruiting of newcomers from outside the system
    D. may not be utilized in *closed* career systems with low maximum age limits for entrance

18. Of the following, the fields in which operating agency personnel offices generally exercise the MOST stringent controls over first line supervisors in the agency are
    A. methods analysis and work simplification
    B. selection and position classification
    C. vestibule training and Gantt chart
    D. suggestion systems and staff development

19. Of the following, computers are normally MOST effective in handling
    A. large masses of data requiring simple processing
    B. small amounts of data requiring constantly changing complex processing
    C. data for which reported values are often subject to inaccuracies
    D. large amounts of data requiring continual programming and reprocessing

20. Contingency planning, which has long been used by the military and is assuming increasing importance in other organizations, may BEST be described as a process which utilizes
    A. alternative plans based on varying assumptions
    B. *crash programs* by organizations departmentalized along process lines
    C. plans which mandate substitution of equipment for manpower at predetermined operational levels
    D. plans that individually and accurately predict future events

21. In the management of inventory, two kinds of costs normally determine when to order and in what amounts.
    The one of the following choices which includes BOTH of these kinds of costs is _____ costs and _____ costs.
    A. carrying; storage
    B. personnel; order
    C. computer; order
    D. personnel; computer

22. At top management levels, the one of the following which is generally the MOST important executive skill is skill in
    A. budgeting procedures
    B. a technical discipline
    C. controlling actions in accordance with previously approved plans
    D. seeing the organization as a whole

23. Of the following, the BEST way to facilitate the successful operation of a committee is to set guidelines establishing its
    A. budget exclusive of personnel costs
    B. location
    C. schedule of meetings or conferences
    D. scope of purpose

24. Executive training programs that single out particular managers and groom them for promotion create the so-called organizational *crown princes*.
    Of the following, the MOST serious problem that arises in connection with this practice is that
    A. the managers chosen for promotion seldom turn out to be the best managers since the future potential of persons cannot be predicted
    B. not enough effort is made to remove organizational obstacles in the way of their development and achievement
    C. the resentment of the managers not selected for the program has an adverse effect on the motivation of those managers not selected
    D. performance appraisal and review are not carried out systematically enough

25. Of the following, the LEAST likely result of the use of the concept of job enlargement is that
    A. coordination will be simplified
    B. the individual's job will become less challenging
    C. worker satisfaction will increase
    D. fewer people will have to give attention to each piece of work

KEY (CORRECT ANSWERS)

1.	C	11.	A
2.	A	12.	C
3.	A	13.	B
4.	C	14.	B
5.	B	15.	D
6.	B	16.	B
7.	C	17.	A
8.	A	18.	B
9.	A	19.	A
10.	C	20.	A

21.	A
22.	D
23.	D
24.	C
25.	B

TEST 2

DIRECTIONS: Each question or incomplete statement is followed by several suggested answers or completions. Select the one that BEST answers the question or completes the statement. *PRINT THE LETTER OF THE CORRECT ANSWER IN THE SPACE AT THE RIGHT.*

1. The one of the following which is MOST likely to be emphasized in the use of the brainstorming technique is the
   A. early consideration of cost factors of all ideas which may be suggested
   B. avoidance of impractical suggestions
   C. separation of the generation of ideas from their evaluation
   D. appraisal of suggestions concurrently with their initial presentation

   1.____

2. Of the following, the BEST method for assessing managerial performance is generally to
   A. compare the manager's accomplishments against clear, specific, agreed-upon goals
   B. compare the manager's traits with those of his peers on a predetermined objective
   C. measure the manager's behavior against a listing of itemized personal traits
   D. measure the manager's success according to the enumeration of the *satisfaction* principle

   2.____

3. As compared with recruitment from outside, selection from within the service must generally show GREATER concern for the
   A. prestige in which the public service as a whole is held by the public
   B. morale of the candidate group compromising the recruitment field
   C. cost of examining per candidate
   D. benefits of the use of standardized and validated tests

   3.____

4. Performance budgeting focuses PRIMARY attention upon which one of the following? The
   A. things to be acquired, such as supplies and equipment
   B. general character and relative importance of the work to be done or the service to be rendered
   C. list of personnel to be employed, by specific title
   D. separation of employee performance evaluations from employee compensation

   4.____

5. Of the following, the FIRST step in the installation and operation of a performance budgeting system generally should be the
   A. identification of program costs in relationship to the accounting system and operating structure
   B. identification of the specific end results of past programs in other jurisdictions

   5.____

C. identification of work programs that are meaningful for management purposes
D. establishment of organizational structures each containing only one work program

6. Of the following, the MOST important purpose of a system of quarterly allotments of appropriated funds generally is to enable the
   A. head of the judicial branch to determine the legality of agency requests for budget increases
   B. operating agencies of government to upgrade the quality of their services without increasing costs
   C. head of the executive branch to control the rate at which the operating agencies obligate and expend funds
   D. operating agencies of government to avoid payment for services which have not been properly rendered by employees

7. In the preparation of the agency's budget, the agency's central budget office has two responsibilities: program review and management improvement. Which one of the following questions concerning an operating agency's program is MOST closely related to the agency budget officer's program review responsibility?
   A. Can expenditures for supplies, materials, or equipment be reduced?
   B. Will improved work methods contribute to a more effective program?
   C. What is the relative importance of this program as compared to a higher level of program performance?
   D. Will a realignment of responsibilities contribute to a higher level of program performance?

8. Of the following, the method of evaluating relative rates of return normally and generally thought to be MOST useful in evaluating government operations is _____ analysis.
   A. cost-benefit
   B. budget variance
   C. investment capital
   D. budget planning program

9. The one of the following assumptions that is LEAST likely to be made by a democratic or permissive type of leader is that
   A. commitment to goals is seldom a result of monetary rewards alone
   B. people can learn not only to accept, but also to seek, responsibility
   C. the average person prefers security over advancement
   D. creativity may be found in most segments of the population

10. In attempting to motivate subordinates, a manager should PRINCIPALLY be aware of the fact that
    A. the psychological qualities of people, in general, are easily predictable
    B. fear, as a traditional form of motivation, has lost much of its former power to motivate people in our modern industrial society
    C. fear is still the most potent force in motivating the behavior of subordinates in the public service
    D. the worker has very little control over the quality and quantity of his output

11. Assume that the following figures represent the number of work-unit that were produced during a week by each of sixteen employees in a division:

    12 16 13 18
    21 12 16 13
    16 13 17 21
    13 15 18 20

    If all of the employees of the division who produced thirteen work-units during the week had instead produced fifteen work-units during that same week, then for that week the
    A. mean, median, and mode would all change
    B. mean and mode would change, but the median would remain the same
    C. mode and median would change, but the mean would remain the same
    D. mode, mean, and median would all still remain unchanged in value

12. An important law in motivation theory is called the *law of effect*. This law says that behavior which satisfies a person's needs tends to be repeated; behavior which does not satisfy a person's needs tends to be eliminated.
    The one of the following which is the BEST interpretation of this law is that
    A. productivity depends on personality traits
    B. diversity of goals leads to instability and motivation
    C. the greater the satisfaction, the more likely it is that the behavior will be reinforced
    D. extrinsic satisfaction is more important than intrinsic reward

13. Of the following, the MOST acceptable reason an administrator can give for taking advice from other employees in the organization only when he asks for it is that he wants to
    A. encourage creativity and high morale
    B. keep dysfunctional pressures and inconsistent recommendations to a minimum
    C. show his superiors and peers who is in charge
    D. show his subordinates who is in charge

14. A complete picture of the communication channels in an organization can BEST be revealed by
    A. observing the planned paperwork system
    B. recording the highly intermittent patterns of communication
    C. plotting the entire flow of information over a period of time
    D. monitoring the *grapevine*

Questions 15-16.

DIRECTIONS: Questions 15 and 16 are to be answered SOLELY on the basis of the following passage.

Management by objectives (MBO) may be defined as the process by which the superior and the subordinate managers of an organization jointly define its common goals, define each individual's major areas of responsibility in terms of the results expected of him and use these measures as guides for operating the unit and assessing the contribution of each of its members.

The MBO approach requires that after organizational goals are established and communicated, targets must be set for each individual position which are congruent with organizational goals. Periodic performance reviews and a final review using the objectives set as criteria are also basic to this approach.

Recent studies have shown that MBO programs are influenced by attitudes and perceptions of the boss, the company, the reward-punishment system, and the program itself. In addition, the manner in which the MBO program is carried out can influence the success of the program. A study done in the late sixties indicates that the best results are obtained when the manager sets goals which deal with significant problem areas in the organizational unit, or with the subordinate's personal deficiencies. These goals must be clear with regard to what is expected of the subordinate. The frequency of feedback is also important in the success of a management-by-objectives program. Generally, the greater the amount of feedback, the more successful the MBO program.

15. According to the above passage, the expected output for individual employees should be determined
    A. after a number of reviews of work performance
    B. after common organizational goals are defined
    C. before common organizational goals are defined
    D. on the basis of an employee's personal qualities

16. According to the above passage, the management-by-objectives approach requires
    A. less feedback than other types of management programs
    B. little review of on-the-job performance after the initial setting of goals
    C. general conformance between individual goals and organizational goals
    D. the setting of goals which deal with minor problem area in the organization

Questions 17-19.

DIRECTIONS: Questions 17 through 19 are to be answered SOLELY on the basis of the following passage.

During the last decade, a great deal of interest has been generated around the phenomenon of organizational development, or the process of developing human resources through conscious organization effort. Organizational development (OD) stresses improving interpersonal relationships and organizational skills, such as communication, to a much greater degree than individual training ever did.

The kind of training that an organization should emphasize depends upon the present and future structure of the organization. If future organizations are to be unstable, shifting coalitions, then individual skills and abilities, particularly those emphasizing innovativeness, creativity, flexibility, and the latest technological knowledge, are crucial, and individual training is most appropriate.

But if there is to be little change in organizational structure, then the main thrust of training should be group-oriented or organizational development. This approach seems better designed for overcoming hierarchical barriers, for developing a degree of interpersonal relationships which make communication along the chain of command possible, and for retaining a modicum of innovation and/or flexibility.

17. According to the above passage, group-oriented training is MOST useful in 17.____
    A. developing a communications system that will facilitate understanding through the chain of command
    B. highly flexible and mobile organizations
    C. preventing the crossing of hierarchical barriers within an organization
    D. saving energy otherwise wasted on developing methods of dealing with rigid hierarchies

18. The one of the following conclusions which can be drawn MOST appropriately from the above passage is that 18.____
    A. behavioral research supports the use of organizational development training method rather than individualized training
    B. it is easier to provide individualized training in specific skills than to set up sensitivity training programs
    C. organizational development eliminates innovative or flexible activity
    D. the nature of an organization greatly influences which training methods will be most effective

19. According to the above passage, the one of the following which is LEAST important for large-scale organizations geared to rapid and abrupt change is 19.____
    A. current technological information
    B. development of a high degree of interpersonal relationships
    C. development of individual skills and abilities
    D. emphasis on creativity

Questions 20-25.

DIRECTIONS: Each of Questions 20 through 25 consist of a statement which contains one word that is incorrectly used because it is not in keeping with the meaning that the quotation is evidently intended to convey. Determine which word is INCORRECTLY used. Select from the choices lettered A, B, C, and D the word which, when substituted for the incorrectly used word, would BEST help to convey the meaning of the statement.

20. One of the considerations likely to affect the currency of classification, particularly in professional and managerial occupations, is the impact of the incumbent's capacities on the job. Some work is highly susceptible to change as the result of the special talents or interests of the classifier. Organization should never be so rigid as not to capitalize on the innovative or unusual proclivities of its key employees. While a machine operator may not be able, even subtly, to change the character or level of his job, the design engineer, the attorney, or the organization and methods analyst might readily do so. Reliance on his judgment and the scope of his assignments may both grow as the result of his skill, insight, and capacity.

    A. unlikely B. incumbent C. directly D. scope

    20.____

21. The supply of services by the state is not governed by market price. The aim is to supply such services to all who need them and to treat all consumers equally. This objective especially compels the civil servant to maintain a role f strict impartiality, based on the principle of equality of individual citizens vis-à-vis their government. However, there is a clear difference between being neutral and impartial. If the requirement is construed to mean that all civil servants should be political eunuchs, devoid of the drive and motivation essential to dynamic administration, then the concept of impartiality is being seriously utilized. Modern governments should not be stopped from demanding that their hirelings have not only the technical but the emotional qualifications necessary for whole-hearted effort.

    A. determined B. rule C. stable D. misapplied

    21.____

22. The manager was barely listening. Recently, at the divisional level, several new fronts of troubles had erupted, including a requirement to increase production yet hold down operating costs and somehow raise quality standards. Though the three objectives were basically obsolete, top departmental management was insisting on the simultaneous attainment of them, an insistence not helping the manager's ulcer, an old enemy within. Thus, the manager could not find time for interest in individuals—only in statistics which regiment of individuals, like unconsidered Army privates, added up to.

    A. quantity B. battalion C. incompatible D. quiet

    22.____

23. When a large volume of data flows directly between operators and first-line supervisors, senior executives tend to be out of the mainstream of work. Summary reports can increase their remoteness. An executive needs to know the volume, quality, and cost of completed work, and exceptional problems. In addition, he may desire information on key operating conditions. Summary reports on these matters are, therefore, essential features of a communications network and make delegation without loss of control possible.

    A. unimportant B. quantity C. offset D. incomplete

    23.____

24. Of major significance in management is harmony between the overall objectives of the organization and the managerial objectives within that organization. In addition, harmony among goals of managers is impossible; they should not be at cross-purposes. Each manager's goal should supplement and assist the goals of his colleagues. Likewise, the objectives of individuals or non-management members should be harmonized with those of the manager. When this is accomplished, genuine teamwork is the result, and human relations are aided materially. The integration of managers' and individuals' goals aids in achieving greater work satisfaction at all levels. 24.____
   A. competition   B. dominate   C. incremental   D. vital

25. Change constantly challenges the manager. Some of this change is evolutionary, some revolutionary, some recognizable, some non-recognizable. Both forces within an enterprise and forces outside the enterprise cause managers to act and react in initiating changes in their immediate working environment. Change invalidates existing operations. Goals are not being accomplished in the best manner, problems develop, and frequently because of the lack of time, only patched-up solutions are followed. The result is that the mode of management is profound in nature and temporary in effectiveness. A complete overhaul of managerial operations should take place. It appears quite likely that we are just beginning to see the real effects of change in our society; the pace probably will accelerate in ways that few really understand or know how to handle. 25.____
   A. confirms   B. decline   C. instituting   D. superficial

KEY (CORRECT ANSWERS)

1.	C		11.	B
2.	A		12.	C
3.	B		13.	B
4.	B		14.	C
5.	C		15.	B
6.	C		16.	C
7.	C		17.	A
8.	A		18.	D
9.	C		19.	B
10.	B		20.	B

21. D
22. C
23. C
24. D
25. D

EXAMINATION SECTION
TEST 1

DIRECTIONS: Each question or incomplete statement is followed by several suggested answers or completions. Select the one that BEST answers the question or completes the statement. *PRINT THE LETTER OF THE CORRECT ANSWER IN THE SPACE AT THE RIGHT.*

1. Assume that a manager is preparing a list of reasons to justify making a major change in methods and procedures in his agency.
   Which of the following reasons would be LEAST appropriate on such a list?
   A. Improve the means for satisfying needs and wants of agency personnel
   B. Increase efficiency
   C. Intensify competition and stimulate loyalty to separate work groups
   D. Contribute to the individual and group satisfaction of agency personnel

   1.____

2. Many managers recognize the benefits of decentralization but are concerned about the danger of over-relaxation of control as a result of increased delegation.
   Of the following, the MOST appropriate means of establishing proper control under decentralization is for the manager to
   A. establish detailed standards for all phases of operation
   B. shift his attention from operating details to appraisal of results
   C. keep himself informed by decreasing the time span covered by reports
   D. make unilateral decisions on difficult situations that arise in decentralized locations

   2.____

3. In some agencies, the counsel to the agency head is given the right to bypass the chain of command and issue orders directly to the staff concerning matters that involve certain specific processes and practices.
   This situation MOST NEARLY illustrates the principle of _____ authority.
   A. the acceptance theory of   B. multiple-linear
   C. splintered   D. functional

   3.____

4. Assume that a manager is writing a brief report to his superior outlining the advantages of matrix organization.
   Of the following, it would be INCORRECT to state that
   A. in matrix organization, a project is emphasized by designating one individual as the focal point for all matters pertaining to it
   B. utilization of manpower can be flexible in matrix organization because a reservoir of specialists is maintained in the line operations
   C. the usual line staff arrangement is generally reversed in matrix organization
   D. in matrix organization, responsiveness to project needs is generally faster due to establishing needed communication lines and decision points

   4.____

5. It is commonly understood that communication is an important part of the administrative process.
Which of the following is NOT a valid principle of the communication process in administration?
   A. The channels of communication should be spontaneous.
   B. The lines of communication should be as direct and as short as possible.
   C. Communications should be authenticated.
   D. The persons serving in communications centers should be competent.

6. The PRIMARY purpose of the quantitative approach in management is to
   A. identify better alternatives for management decision-making
   B. substitute data for judgment
   C. match opinions to data
   D. match data to opinions

7. If an executive wants to make a strong case for running his agency as a flat type of structure, he should point out that the PRIMARY advantage of doing so is to
   A. provide less experience in decision-making for agency personnel
   B. facilitate frequent contact between each superior and his immediate subordinates
   C. improve communication and unify attitudes
   D. improve communication and diversify attitudes

8. In deciding how detailed his delegation of authority to a subordinate should be, a manager should follow the general principle that
   A. delegation of authority is more detailed at the top of the organizational structure
   B. detailed delegation of authority is associated with detailed work assignments
   C. delegation of authority should be in sufficient detail to prevent overlapping assignments
   D. detailed delegation of authority is associated with broad work assignments

9. In recent years, newer and more fluid types of organizational forms have been developed. One of these is a type of free-form organization.
Another name for this type of organization is the
   A. project organization   B. semimix organization
   C. naturalistic structure   D. semipermanent structure

10. Which of the following is the MAJOR objective of operational or management systems audits?
    A. Determining the number of personnel needed
    B. Recommending opportunities for improving operating and management practices
    C. Detecting fraud
    D. Determining organization problems

11. Assume that a manager observes that conflict exists between his agency and another operating agency of government.
    Which of the following statements is the LEAST probable cause of this conflict?
    A. Incompatibility between the agencies' goals but similarity in their resource allocations
    B. Compatibility between agencies' goals and resources
    C. Status differences between agency personnel
    D. Differences in perceptions of each other's policies

12. Of the following, a MAJOR purpose of brainstorming as a problem-solving technique is to
    A. develop the ability to concentrate
    B. encourage creative thinking
    C. evaluate employees' ideas
    D. develop critical ability

13. The one of the following requirements which is LEAST likely to accompany regular delegation of work from a manager to a subordinate is a(n)
    A. need to review the organization's workload
    B. indication of what work the subordinate is to do
    C. need to grant authority to the subordinate
    D. obligation for the subordinate who accepts the work to try to complete it

14. Of the following, the one factor which is generally considered LEAST essential to successful committee operation is
    A. stating a clear definition of the authority and scope of the committee
    B. selecting the committee chairman carefully
    C. limiting the size of the committee to four persons
    D. limiting the subject matter to that which can be handled in group discussion

15. In using the program evaluation and review technique, the *critical path* is the path that
    A. requires the shortest time
    B. requires the longest time
    C. focuses most attention on social constraints
    D. focuses most attention to repetitious jobs

16. Which one of the following is LEAST characteristic of the management-by-objectives approach?
    A. The scope within which the employee may exercise decision-making is broadened.
    B. The employee starts with a self-appraisal of his performances, abilities, and potential.
    C. Emphasis is placed on activities performed; activities orientation is maximized.
    D. Each employee participates in determining his own objectives.

17. The function of management which puts into effect the decisions, plans, and programs that have previously been worked out for achieving the goals of the group is MOST appropriately called
    A. scheduling   B. classifying   C. budgeting   D. directing

18. In the establishment of a plan to improve office productive efficiency, which of the following guidelines is LEAST helpful in setting sound work standards?
    A. Employees must accept the plan's objectives.
    B. Current production averages must be promulgated as work standards for a group.
    C. The work flow must generally be fairly constant.
    D. The operation of the plan must be expressed in terms understandable to the worker.

19. The one of the following activities which, generally speaking, is of *relatively* MAJOR importance at the lower-management level and of *somewhat* LESSER importance at higher-management levels is
    A. actuating   B. forecasting   C. organizing   D. planning

20. Three styles of leadership exist: democratic, authoritarian, and laissez-faire. Of the following work situations, the one in which a democratic approach would normally be the MOST effective is when the work is
    A. routine and moderately complex   B. repetitious and simple
    C. complex and not routine   D. simple and not routine

21. Governmental and business organizations *generally* encounter the GREATEST difficulties in developing tangible measures of which one of the following?
    A. The level of expenditures   B. Contributions to social welfare
    C. Retention rates   D. Causes of labor unrest

22. Of the following, a *management-by-objectives* program is BEST described as
    A. a new comprehensive plan of organization
    B. introduction of budgets and financial controls
    C. introduction of long-range planning
    D. development of future goals with supporting and related progress reviews

23. Research and analysis is probably the most widely used technique for selecting alternatives when major planning decisions are involved.
    Of the following, a VALUABLE characteristic of research and analysis is that this technique
    A. places the problem in a meaningful conceptual framework
    B. involves practical application of the various alternatives
    C. accurately analyzes all important tangibles
    D. is much less expensive than other problem-solving methods

24. If a manager were assigned the task of using a systems approach to designing 24.____
a new work unit, which of the following should he consider FIRST in carrying
out his design?
    A. Networks
    B. Work flows and information processes
    C. Linkages and relationships
    D. Decision points and control loops

25. The MAIN distinction between Theory X and Theory Y approaches to 25.____
organization, in accordance with Douglas McGregor's view, is that Theory Y
    A. considers that work is natural to people; Theory X assumes that people
       are lazy and avoid work
    B. leads to a tall, narrow organization structure, while Theory X leads to one
       that is flat
    C. organizations motivate people with money; Theory X organizations
       motivate people with good working conditions
    D. represents authoritarian management, while Theory X management is
       participative

KEY (CORRECT ANSWERS)

1.	C		11.	B
2.	B		12.	B
3.	D		13.	A
4.	C		14.	C
5.	A		15.	B
6.	A		16.	C
7.	C		17.	D
8.	B		18.	B
9.	A		19.	A
10.	B		20.	C

21.	B
22.	D
23.	A
24.	B
25.	A

TEST 2

DIRECTIONS: Each question or incomplete statement is followed by several suggested answers or completions. Select the one that BEST answers the question or completes the statement. *PRINT THE LETTER OF THE CORRECT ANSWER IN THE SPACE AT THE RIGHT.*

1. Of the following, the stage in decision-making which is usually MOST difficult is
   A. stating the alternatives
   B. predicting the possible outcome of each alternative
   C. evaluating the relative merits of each alternative
   D. minimizing the undesirable aspects of the alternative selected

   1.____

2. In a department where a clerk is reporting both to a senior clerk in charge of the mail room and also to a supervising clerk in charge of the duplicating section, there may be a breakdown of the management principle called
   A. horizontal specialization   B. job enrichment
   C. unity of command   D. Graicunas' Law

   2.____

3. Of the following, the failure by line managers to accept and appreciate the benefits and limitations of a new program or system VERY frequently can be traced to the
   A. budgetary problems involved
   B. resultant need to reduce staff
   C. lack of controls it engenders
   D. failure of top management to support its implementation

   3.____

4. Although there is general agreement that *management-by-objectives* has made a major contribution to modern management of large organizations, criticisms of the system during the past few years have resulted in
   A. mounting pressure for relaxation of management goals
   B. renewed concern with human values and the manager's personal needs
   C. over-mechanistic application of the perceptions of the behavioral scientists
   D. disillusionment with *management-by-objectives* on the part of a majority of managers

   4.____

5. Of the following, which is usually considered to be a MAJOR obstacle to the systematic analysis of potential problems by managers?
   A. Managers have a tendency to think that all the implications of some proposed step cannot be fully understood.
   B. Rewards rarely go to those managers who are most successful at resolving current problems in management.
   C. There is a common conviction of manages that their goals are difficult to achieve.
   D. Managers are far more concerned about correcting today's problems than with preventing tomorrow's.

   5.____

6. Which of the following should generally have the MOST influence on the selection of supervisors?
    A. Experience within the work unit where the vacancies exist
    B. Amount of money needed to effect the promotion
    C. Personal preferences of the administration
    D. Evaluation of capacity to exercise supervisory responsibilities

7. In questioning a potential administrator for selection purposes, the one of the following practices which is MOST desirable is to
    A. encourage the job applicant to give primarily *yes* or *no* replies
    B. get the applicant to talk freely and in detail about his background
    C. let the job applicant speak most of the time
    D. probe the applicant's attitudes, motivation, and willingness to accept responsibility

8. In implementing the managerial function of training subordinates, it is USEFUL to know that a widely agreed-upon definition of human learning is that learning
    A. is a relatively permanent change in behavior that results from reinforced practice or experience
    B. involves an improvement, but not necessarily a change in behavior
    C. involves a change in behavior, but not necessarily an improvement
    D. is a temporary change in behavior which must be subject to practice or experience

9. If a manager were thinking about using a committee of subordinates to solve an operating problem, which of the following would generally NOT be an advantage of such use of the committee approach?
    A. Improved coordination   B. Low cost
    C. Increased motivation   D. Integrated judgment

10. Which one of the following management approaches MOST often uses model-building techniques to solve management problems?
    _____ approach.
    A. Behavioral   B. Fiscal   C. Quantitative   D. Process

11. Of the following, the MOST serious risk in using budgets as a tool for management control is the
    A. probable neglect of other good management practices
    B. likelihood of guesswork because of the need to plan far in advance
    C. possibility of undue emphasis on factors that are easiest to measure
    D. danger of making qualitative rather than quantitative assessments of performance

12. In government budgeting, the problem of relating financial transactions to the fiscal year in which they are budgeted is BEST met by
    A. determining the cash balance by comparing how much money has been received and how much has been paid out
    B. applying net revenue to the fiscal year in which they are collected as offset by relevant expenses

C. adopting a system whereby appropriations are entered when they are received and expenditures are entered when they are paid out
D. entering expenditures on the books when the obligation to make the expenditure is made

13. If the agency's bookkeeping system records income when it is received and expenditures when the money is paid out this system is USUALLY known as a _____ system.
    A. cash
    B. flow-payment
    C. deferred
    D. fiscal year income

14. An audit, as the term applies to budget execution, is MOST NEARLY a
    A. procedure based on the budget estimates
    B. control exercised by the executive on the legislature in the establishment of program priorities
    C. check on the legality of expenditures and is based on the appropriations act
    D. requirement which must be met before funds can be spent

15. In government budgeting, there is a procedure known as *allotment.*
    Of the following statements which relate to allotment, select the one that is MOST generally considered to be correct.
    Allotment
    A. increases the practice of budget units coming back to the legislature branch for supplemental appropriations
    B. is simply an example of red tape
    C. eliminates the requirement of timing of expenditures
    D. is designed to prevent waste

16. In government budgeting, the establishment of the schedules of allotments is MOST generally the responsibility of the
    A. budget unit and the legislature
    B. budget unit and the executive
    C. budget unit only
    D. executive and the legislature

17. Of the following statements relating to preparation of an organization's budget request, which is the MOST generally valid precaution?
    A. Give specific instructions on the format or budget requests and required supporting data
    B. Because of the complexity of preparing a budget request, avoid argumentation to support the requests
    C. Put requests in whatever format is desirable
    D. Consider that final approval will be given to initial estimates

18. Of the following statements which relate to the budget process in a well-organized government, select the one that is MOST NEARLY correct.
    A. The budget cycle is the step-by-step process which is repeated each and every fiscal year.
    B. Securing approval of the budget does not take place within the budget cycle.

C. The development of a new budget and putting it into effect is a two-step process known as the budget cycle.
D. The fiscal period, usually a fiscal year, has no relation to the budget cycle.

19. If a manager were asked what PPBS stands for, he would be RIGHT if he said _____ budgeting system.
    A. public planning
    B. planning programming
    C. planning projections
    D. programming procedures

Questions 20-21.

DIRECTIONS: Questions 20 and 21 are to be answered on the basis of the following information.

Sample Budget

Refuse Collection	Amount
Personal Services	$30,000
Contractual Services	5,000
Supplies and Materials	5,000
Capital Outlay	10,000
	$50,000

Residential Collections	
Dwellings – 1 pickup per week	1,000
Tons of refuse collected per year	375
Cost of collections per ton	$ 8
Cost per dwelling pickup per year	$ 3
Total annual cost	$3,000

20. The sample budget shown is a simplified example of a _____ budget.
    A. factorial   B. performance   C. qualitative   D. rational

21. The budget shown in the sample differs CHIEFLY from line-item and program budgets in that it includes
    A. objects of expenditure but not activities or functions
    B. only activities, functions, and control
    C. activities and functions but not objects of expenditures
    D. levels of service

Question 22.

DIRECTIONS: Question 22 is to be answered on the basis of the following information.

Sample Budget

Environmental Safety
  Air Pollution Protection
    Personal Services $20,000,000
    Contractual Services   4,000,000
    Supplies and Materials   4,000,000
    Capital Outlay   2,000,000
    Total Air Pollution Protection $30,000,000

  Water Pollution Protection
    Personal Services $23,000,000
    Supplies and Materials   4,500,000
    Capital Outlay   20,500,000
    Total Water Pollution Protection $48,000,000

Total Environmental Safety $78,000,000

22. Based on the above budget, which is the MOST valid statement?
    A. Environmental Safety, Air Pollution Protection, and Water Pollution Protection could all be considered program elements.
    B. The object listings included water pollution protection and capital outlay.
    C. Examples of the program element listings in the above are personal services and supplies and materials
    D. Contractual Services and Environmental Safety were the program element listings.

23. Which of the following is NOT an advantage of a program budget over a line-item budget?
A program budget
    A. allows us to set up priority lists in deciding what activities we will spend our money on
    B. gives us more control over expenditures than a line-item budget
    C. is more informative in that we know the broad purposes of spending money
    D. enables us to see if one program is getting much less money than the others

24. If a manager were trying to explain the fundamental difference between traditional accounting theory and practice and the newer practice of managerial accounting, he would be MOST accurate if he said that
    A. traditional accounting practice focused on providing information for persons outside organizations, while managerial accounting focuses on providing information for people inside organizations
    B. traditional accounting practice focused on providing information for persons inside organizations while managerial accounting focuses on providing information for persons outside organizations

C. managerial accounting is exclusively concerned with historical facts while traditional accounting stresses future projections exclusively
D. traditional accounting practice is more budget-focused than managerial accounting

25. Which of the following formulas is used to determine the number of days required to process work?
_____ = Days to Process Work

A. $\dfrac{\text{Employees} \times \text{Daily Output}}{\text{Volume}}$

B. $\dfrac{\text{Volume} \times \text{Daily Output}}{\text{Volume}}$

C. $\dfrac{\text{Volume}}{\text{Employees} \times \text{Daily Output}}$

D. $\dfrac{\text{Employees} \times \text{Volume}}{\text{Daily Output}}$

25.____

KEY (CORRECT ANSWERS)

1.	C		11.	C
2.	C		12.	D
3.	D		13.	A
4.	B		14.	C
5.	D		15.	D
6.	D		16.	C
7.	D		17.	A
8.	A		18.	A
9.	B		19.	B
10.	C		20.	B

21. D
22. A
23. B
24. A
25. C

TEST 3

DIRECTIONS: Each question or incomplete statement is followed by several suggested answers or completions. Select the one that BEST answers the question or completes the statement. *PRINT THE LETTER OF THE CORRECT ANSWER IN THE SPACE AT THE RIGHT.*

1. Electronic data processing equipment can produce more information faster than can be generated by any other means.
   In view of this, the MOST important problem faced by management at present is to
   A. keep computers fully occupied
   B. find enough computer personnel
   C. assimilate and properly evaluate the information
   D. obtain funds to establish appropriate information systems

   1.____

2. A well-designed management information system ESSENTIALLY provides each executive and manager the information he needs for
   A. determining computer time requirements
   B. planning and measuring results
   C. drawing a new organization chart
   D. developing a new office layout

   2.____

3. It is generally agreed that management policies should be periodically reappraised and restated in accordance with current conditions.
   Of the following, the approach which would be MOST effective in determining whether a policy should be revised is to
   A. conduct interviews with staff members at all levels in order to ascertain the relationship between the policy and actual practice
   B. make proposed revisions in the policy and apply it to current problems
   C. make up hypothetical situations using both the old policy and a revised version in order to make comparisons
   D. call a meeting of top level staff in order to discuss ways of revising the policy

   3.____

4. Every manager has many occasions to lead a conference or participate in a conference of some sort.
   Of the following statements that pertain to conferences and conference leadership, which is generally considered to be MOST valid?
   A. Since World War II, the trend has been toward fewer shared decisions and more conferences.
   B. The most important part of a conference leader's job is to direct discussion.
   C. In providing opportunities for group interaction, management should avoid consideration of its past management philosophy.
   D. A good administrator cannot lead a good conference if he is a poor public speaker.

   4.____

5. Of the following, it is usually LEAST desirable for a conference leader to
   A. turn the question to the person who asked it
   B. summarize proceedings periodically
   C. make a practice of not repeating questions
   D. ask a question without indicating who is to reply

6. The behavioral school of management thought bases its beliefs on certain assumptions.
   Which of the following is NOT a belief of this school of thought?
   A. People tend to seek and accept responsibility.
   B. Most people can be creative in solving problems.
   C. People prefer security above all else.
   D. Commitment is the most important factor in motivating people.

7. The one of the following objectives which would be LEAST appropriate as a major goal of research in the field of human resources management is to
   A. predict future conditions, events, and manpower needs
   B. evaluate established policies, programs, and practices
   C. evaluate proposed policies, programs, and practices
   D. identify deficient organizational units and apply suitable penalties

8. Of the following general interviewing methods or techniques, the one that is USUALLY considered to be effective in counseling, grievances, and appraisal interviews is the _____ interview.
   A. directed   B. non-directed   C. panel   D. patterned

9. The ESSENTIAL first phase of decision-making is
   A. finding alternative solutions
   B. making a diagnosis of the problem
   C. selecting the plan to follow
   D. analyzing and comparing alternative solutions

10. Assume that, in a certain organization, a situation has developed in which there is little difference in status or authority between individuals.
    Which of the following would be the MOST likely result with regard to communication in this organization?
    A. Both the accuracy and flow of communication will be improved.
    B. Both the accuracy and flow of communication will substantially decrease.
    C. Employees will seek more formal lines of communication.
    D. Neither the flow nor the accuracy of communication will be improved over the former hierarchical structure.

11. The main function of many agency administrative offices is *information management*. Information that is received by an administrative officer may be classified as active or passive, depending upon whether or not it requires the recipient to take some action.

Of the following, the item received which is clearly the MOST active information is
- A. an appointment of a new staff member
- B. a payment voucher for a new desk
- C. a press release concerning a past city event
- D. the minutes of a staff meeting

12. Which one of the following sets BEST describes the general order in which to teach an operation to a new employee?
    - A. Prepare, present, tryout, follow-up
    - B. Prepare, test, tryout, re-test
    - C. Present, test, tryout, follow-up
    - D. Test, present, follow-up, re-test

13. Of the following, public employees may be separated from public service
    - A. for the same reasons which are generally acceptable for discharging employees in private industry
    - B. only under the most trying circumstances
    - C. under procedures that are neither formalized nor subject to review
    - D. solely in extreme cases involving offenses of gravest character

14. Of the following, the one LEAST considered to be a communication barrier is
    - A. group feedback
    - B. charged words
    - C. selective perception
    - D. symbolic meanings

15. Of the following ways for a manager to handle his appointments, the BEST way, according to experts in administration, generally is to
    - A. schedule his own appointments and inform his secretary not to reserve his time without his approval
    - B. encourage everyone to make appointments through his secretary and tell her when he makes his own appointments
    - C. see no one who has not made a previous appointment
    - D. permit anyone to see him without an appointment

16. Assume that a manager decides to examine closely one of five units under his supervision to uncover problems common to all five.
    His research technique is MOST closely related to the method called
    - A. experimentation
    - B. simulation
    - C. linear analysis
    - D. sampling

17. If one views the process of management as a dynamic process, which one of the following functions is NOT a legitimate part of that process?
    - A. Communication
    - B. Decision-making
    - C. Organizational slack
    - D. Motivation

18. Which of the following would be the BEST statement of a budget-oriented purpose for a government administrator? To
    A. provide 200 hours of instruction in basic reading for 3,500 adult illiterates at a cost of $1 million in the next fiscal year
    B. inform the public of adult educational programs
    C. facilitate the transfer to a city agency of certain functions of a federally-funded program which is being phased out
    D. improve the reading skills of the adult citizens in the city

19. Modern management philosophy and practices are changing to accommodate the expectations and motivations of organization personnel.
    Which of the following terms INCORRECTLY describes these newer managerial approaches?
    A. Rational management
    B. Participative management
    C. Decentralization
    D. Democratic supervision

20. Management studies support the hypothesis that, in spite of the tendency of employees to censor the information communicated to their supervisor, subordinates are MORE likely to communicate problem-oriented information upward when they have
    A. a long period of service in the organization
    B. a high degree of trust in the supervisor
    C. a high educational level
    D. low status on the organizational ladder

KEY (CORRECT ANSWERS)

1.	C	11.	A
2.	B	12.	A
3.	A	13.	A
4.	B	14.	A
5.	A	15.	B
6.	C	16.	D
7.	D	17.	C
8.	B	18.	A
9.	B	19.	A
10.	D	20.	B

EXAMINATION SECTION
TEST 1

DIRECTIONS: Each question or incomplete statement is followed by several suggested answers or completions. Select the one that BEST answers the question or completes the statement. *PRINT THE LETTER OF THE CORRECT ANSWER IN THE SPACE AT THE RIGHT.*

1. Which one of the following is LEAST likely to be an area or cause of trouble in the use of staff personnel?

    A. Misunderstanding of the role the staff personnel are supposed to play as a result of vagueness of definition of their duties and authority
    B. Tendency of staff personnel almost always to be older than line personnel at comparable salary levels with whom they must deal
    C. Selection of staff personnel who fail to have simultaneously both competence in their specialities and skill in staff work
    D. The staff person fails to understand mixed staff and operating duties

1._____

2. Which of the following is generally NOT a valid statement with respect to the supervisory process?

    A. General supervision is more effective than close supervision.
    B. Employee-centered supervisors lead more effectively than do production-centered supervisors.
    C. Employee satisfaction is directly related to productivity.
    D. Low-producing supervisors use techniques that are different from high-producing supervisors.

2._____

3. Which of the following is the MOST essential element for proper evaluation of the performance of subordinate supervisors?

    A. Careful definition of each supervisor's specific job responsibilities and of his progress in meeting mutually agreed upon work goals
    B. System of rewards and penalties based on each supervisor's progress in meeting clearly defined performance standards
    C. Definition of personality traits, such as industry, initiative, dependability, and cooperativeness, required for effective job performance
    D. Breakdown of each supervisor's job into separate components and a rating of his performance on each individual task

3._____

4. The PRINCIPAL advantage of specialization for the operating efficiency of a public service agency is that specialization

    A. reduces the amount of red tape in coordinating the activities of mutually dependent departments
    B. simplifies the problem of developing adequate job controls
    C. provides employees with a clear understanding of the relationship of their activities to the overall objectives of the agency
    D. reduces destructive competition for power between departments

4._____

5. A list of conditions which encourages good morale inside a work group would NOT include a

   A. high rate of agreement among group members on values and objectives
   B. tight control system to minimize the risk of individual error
   C. good possibility that joint action will accomplish goals
   D. past history of successful group accomplishment

6. Of the following, the MOST important factor to be considered in selecting a training strategy or program is the

   A. requirements of the job to be performed by the trainees
   B. educational level or prior training of the trainees
   C. size of the training group
   D. quality and competence of available training specialists

7. Of the following, the one which is considered to be LEAST characteristic of the higher ranks of management is

   A. that higher levels of management benefit from modern technology
   B. that success is measured by the extent to which objectives are achieved
   C. the number of subordinates that directly report to a manager
   D. the de-emphasis of individual and specialized performance

8. Assume that a manager is preparing a training syllabus to be used in training members of her staff.
   Which of the following would NOT be a valid principle of the learning process to consider when preparing this training syllabus?

   A. When a person has thoroughly learned a task, it takes a lot of effort to create a little more improvement.
   B. In complicated learning situations, there is a period in which an additional period of practice produces an equal amount of improvement in learning.
   C. The less a person knows about the task, the slower the initial progress.
   D. The more a person knows about the task, the slower the initial progress.

9. Which statement BEST illustrates when collective bargaining agreements are working well?

   A. Executives strongly support subordinate managers.
   B. The management rights clause in the contract is clear and enforced.
   C. Contract provisions are competently interpreted.
   D. The provisions of the agreement are properly interpreted, communicated, and observed.

10. An executive who wishes to encourage subordinates to communicate freely with him about a job-related problem should FIRST

    A. state his own position on the problem before listening to the subordinates' ideas
    B. invite subordinates to give their own opinions on the problem
    C. ask subordinates for their reactions to his own ideas about the problem
    D. guard the confidentiality of management information about the problem

11. The ability to deal constructively with intra-organizational conflict is an essential attribute of the successful manager.
The one of the following types of conflict which would be LEAST difficult to handle constructively is a situation in which there is

    A. agreement on objectives, but disagreement as to the probable results of adopting the various alternatives
    B. agreement on objectives, disagreement on alternative courses of action, and relative certainty as to the outcome of one of the alternatives
    C. disagreement on objectives and on alternative courses of action, and relative certainty as to the outcome of one of the alternatives
    D. disagreement on objectives and on alternative courses of action, but uncertainty as to the outcome of the alternatives

12. Which of the following actions does NOT belong in a properly conducted grievance handling process?

    A. Gathering relevant information on why the grievance arose
    B. Formulating a personal judgment about the fairness or unfairness of the grievance at the time the grievance is presented
    C. Establishing tentative answers to the grievance
    D. Following up to see whether the solution has eliminated the difficulty

13. Grievances are generally defined as complaints expressed over work-related matters.
Which one of the following is MOST important for managers to be aware of in connection with this definition?
The

    A. fact that the definition fails to separate the subject of the grievance from the attitude of the grievant
    B. fact that anything in the organization may be the source of the grievance
    C. need to assume that dissatisfied people have adverse effects on productivity
    D. implication that management should be concerned about expressed grievances and unconcerned about unexpressed grievances

14. In carrying out disciplinary action, the MOST important procedure for all managers to follow is to

    A. convince all levels of management on the need for discipline from the organization's viewpoint
    B. follow up on a disciplinary action and not assume that the action has been effective
    C. convince all executives that proper discipline is a legitimate tool for their use
    D. convince all executives that they need to display confidence in the organization's rules

15. Assume that an employee under your supervision is acquitted in court of criminal charges arising out of his employment.
    Of the following statements concerning disciplinary action, which is MOST NEARLY correct?

    A. Disciplinary proceedings against the employee may not be held for the same offenses on which he was tried and acquitted.
    B. In a disciplinary action, the acquittal dispenses with the requirement that the employee be advised as to his constitutional rights.
    C. Civil Rights Law Section 79 prohibits the taking of any further punitive action by an employer if the offense did not involve official corruption.
    D. It is possible for the employee to be found guilty of the same offense when tried in a departmental hearing.

16. Work rules can be an effective tool in the process of personnel management.
    The BEST practical definition for work rules is that they are

    A. minimum standards of conduct or performance that apply to individuals or groups at work in an organization
    B. prescriptions that serve to specialize employee behavior
    C. predetermined decisions about disciplinary action
    D. the major determinant of an organization's climate and the morale of its workforce

Questions 17-18

DIRECTIONS: Questions 17 and 18 pertain to identification of words that are incorrectly used because they are not in keeping with the meaning of the quotation. In answering each question, the first step is to read the passage and identify the incorrectly used word, and then select the word which, when substituted, BEST serves to convey the meaning of the quotation.

17. Among the Housing Manager's overall responsibilities in administering a project is the prevention of the development of conditions which might lead to termination of tenancy and eviction of a tenant. Where there appears to be doubt that a tenant is fully aware of his responsibilities and is thus jeopardizing his tenancy, the Housing Manager should acquaint him with these responsibilities. Where a situation involves behavior of a tenant or a member of his family, the Housing Manager should confirm, through discussions and referrals to social agencies, correction of the conditions before they reach a state where there is no alternative but termination proceedings.

   A. Coordinate
   B. Identify
   C. Assert
   D. Attempt

   17._____

18. The one universal administrative complaint is that the budget is inadequate. Between adequacy and inadequacy lie all degrees of adequacy. Further, human wants are modest in relation to human resources. From these two facts we may conclude that the fundamental criterion of administrative decision must be a criterion of efficiency (the degree to which the goals have been reached relative to the available resources) rather than a criterion of adequacy (the degree to which its goals have been reached). The task of the manager is to maximize social values relative to limited resources.

   A. Improve
   B. Simple
   C. Limitless
   D. Optimize

   18._____

Questions 19-21.

DIRECTIONS: Questions 19 through 21 are to be answered SOLELY on the basis of the following situation.

John Foley, a top administrator, is responsible for output in his organization. Because productivity had been lagging for two periods in a row, Foley decided to establish a committee of his subordinate managers to investigate the reasons for the poor performance and to make recommendations for improvements. After two meetings, the committee came to the conclusions and made the recommendations that follow.

Output forecasts had been handed down from the top without prior consultation with middle management and first level supervision. Lines of authority and responsibility had been unclear. The planning and control process should be decentralized.

After receiving the committee's recommendations, Foley proceeded to take the following actions. Foley decided he would retain final authority to establish quotas but would delegate to the middle managers the responsibility for meeting quotas.

After receiving Foley's decision, the middle managers proceeded to delegate to the first-line supervisors the authority to establish their own quotas. The middle managers eventually received and combined the first-line supervisors' quotas so that these conformed to Foley's.

19. Foley's decision to delegate responsibility for meeting quotas to the middle managers is inconsistent with sound management principles because

    A. Foley should not have involved himself in the first place
    B. middle managers do not have the necessary skills
    C. quotas should be established by the chief executive
    D. responsibility should not be delegated

20. The principle of co-extensiveness of responsibility and authority bears on Foley's decision.
    In this case, it implies that

    A. authority should exceed responsibility
    B. authority should be delegated to match the degree of responsibility
    C. both authority and responsibility should be retained and not delegated
    D. responsibility should be delegated, but authority should be retained

21. The middle managers' decision to delegate to the first-line supervisors the authority to establish quotas was INCORRECTLY reasoned because

    A. delegation and control must go together
    B. first-line supervisors are in no position to establish quotas
    C. one cannot delegate authority that one does not possess
    D. the meeting of quotas should not be delegated

22. If one attempts to list the advantages of the management-by-exception principle as it is used in connection with the budgeting process, several distinct advantages could be cited.
    Which of the following is NOT an advantage of this principle as it applies to the budgeting process?
    Management-by-exception

    A. saves time
    B. identifies critical problem areas
    C. focuses attention and concentrates effort
    D. escalates the frequency and importance of budget-related decisions

23. The MOST accurate description of a budget is that

    A. a budget is made up by an organization to plan its future activities
    B. a budget specifies in dollars and cents how much is spent in a particular time period
    C. a budget specifies how much the organization to which it relates estimates it will spend over a certain period of time
    D. all plans dealing with money are budgets

24. Of the following, the one which is NOT a contribution that a budget makes to organizational programming is that a budget

    A. enables a comparison of what actually happened with what was expected
    B. stresses the need to forecast specific goals and eliminates the need to focus on tasks needed to accomplish goals
    C. may illustrate duplication of effort between interdependent activities
    D. shows the relationship between various organizational segments

25. A line-item budget is a good control budget because

    A. it clearly specifies how the items being purchased will be used
    B. expenditures can be shown primarily for contractual services
    C. it clearly specifies what the money is buying
    D. it clearly specifies the services to be provided

KEY (CORRECT ANSWERS)

1.	B	11.	B
2.	C	12.	B
3.	A	13.	C
4.	B	14.	B
5.	B	15.	D
6.	A	16.	A
7.	A	17.	D
8.	D	18.	C
9.	D	19.	D
10.	B	20.	B

21. C
22. D
23. C
24. B
25. C

TEST 2

DIRECTIONS: Each question or incomplete statement is followed by several suggested answers or completions. Select the one that BEST answers the question or completes the statement. *PRINT THE LETTER OF THE CORRECT ANSWER IN THE SPACE AT THE RIGHT.*

1. The insights of Chester I. Barnard have influenced the development of management thought in significant ways. He is MOST closely identified with a position that has become known as the

    A. acceptance theory of authority
    B. principle of the manager's or executive's span of control
    C. *Theory X* and *Theory Y* dichotomy
    D. unit of command principle

    1._____

2. Certain conditions should exist to insure that a subordinate will decide to accept a communication as being authoritative.
   Which of the following is LEAST valid as a condition which should exist?

    A. The subordinate understands the communication.
    B. At the time of the subordinate's decision, he views the communication as consistent with the organization's purpose and his personal interest.
    C. At the time of the subordinate's decision, he views the communication as more consistent with his personal purposes than with the organization's interest.
    D. The subordinate is mentally and physically able to comply with the communication.

    2._____

3. In exploring the effects that employee participation has on implementing changes in work methods, certain relationships have been established between participation and productivity.
   It has MOST generally been found that highest productivity occurs in groups provided with

    A. participation in the process of change only through representatives of their group
    B. no participation in the change process
    C. full participation in the change process
    D. intermittent participation in the process of change

    3._____

4. The trend LEAST likely to occur in the area of employee-management relations is that

    A. employees will exert more influence on decisions affecting their interests
    B. technological change will have a stronger impact on organizations' human resources
    C. labor will judge management according to company profits
    D. government will play a larger role in balancing the interests of the parties in labor-management affairs

    4._____

5. Members of an organization must satisfy several fundamental psychological needs in order to be happy and productive.
   The BROADEST and MOST basic needs are

   A. achievement, recognition, and acceptance
   B. competition, recognition, and accomplishment
   C. salary increments and recognition
   D. acceptance of competition and economic award

6. Morale has been defined as the capacity of a group of people to pull together steadily for a common purpose.
   Morale thus defined is MOST generally dependent on

   A. job security
   B. group and individual self-confidence
   C. organizational efficiency
   D. physical health of the individuals

7. Which is the CORRECT order of steps to follow when revising office procedure?
   To

   I. develop the improved method as determined by time and motion studies and effective workplace layout
   II. find out how the task is now performed
   III. apply the new method
   IV. analyze the current method

   The CORRECT answer is:
   A. IV, II, I, III
   B. II, I, III, IV
   C. I, II, IV, III
   D. II, IV, I, III

8. In contrast to broad spans of control, narrow spans of control are MOST likely to

   A. provide opportunity for more personal contact between superior and subordinate
   B. encourage decentralization
   C. stress individual initiative
   D. foster group of team effort

9. A manager is coaching a subordinate on the nature of decision-making. She could BEST define decision-making as

   A. choosing between alternatives
   B. making diagnoses of feasible ends
   C. making diagnoses of feasible means
   D. comparing alternatives

10. Of the following, the LEAST valid purpose of an organizational policy statement is to

    A. keep personnel from performing improper actions and functions on routine matters
    B. prevent the mishandling of non-routine matters
    C. provide management personnel with a tool that precludes the need for their use of judgment
    D. provide standard decisions and approaches in handling problems of a recurrent nature

11. Current thinking on bureaucratic organizations is that

    A. bureaucracy is on the way out
    B. bureaucracy, though not perfect, is unlikely to be replaced
    C. bureaucratic organizations are most effective in dealing with constant change
    D. bureaucratic organizations are most effective when dealing with sophisticated customers or clients

12. The development of alternate plans as a major step in planning will normally result in the planner's having several possible course of action available. GENERALLY, this is

    A. *desirable* since such development helps to determine the most suitable alternative and to provide for the unexpected
    B. *desirable* since such development makes the use of planning premises and constraints unnecessary
    C. *undesirable* since the planners should formulate only one way of achieving given goals at a given time
    D. *undesirable* since such action restricts efforts to modify the planning to take advantage of opportunities

13. Assume a manager carries out his responsibilities to his staff according to what is now known about managerial leadership.
    Which of the following statements would MOST accurately reflect his assumptions about proper management?

    A. Efficiency in operations results from allowing the human element to participate in a minimal way.
    B. Efficient operation results from balancing work considerations with personnel considerations.
    C. Efficient operation results from a work force committed to its self-interest.
    D. Efficient operation results from staff relationships that produce a friendly work climate.

14. Assume that a manager is called upon to conduct a management audit. To do this properly, he would have to take certain steps in a specific sequence. Which step should this manager take FIRST?

    A. Managerial performance must be surveyed.
    B. A method of reporting must be established.
    C. Management auditing procedures and documentation must be developed.
    D. Criteria for the audit must be established.

14.____

15. If a manager is required to conduct a scientific investigation of an organizational problem, the FIRST step he should take is to

    A. state his assumptions about the problem
    B. carry out a search for background information
    C. choose the right approach to investigate the validity of his assumptions
    D. define and state the problem

15.____

16. A manager would be correct to assert that the principle of delegation states that decisions should be made PRIMARILY

    A. by persons in an executive capacity qualified to make them
    B. by persons in a non-executive capacity
    C. at as low an organizational level of authority as practicable
    D. by the next lower level of authority

16.____

17. Of the following, which one is NOT regarded by management authorities as a fundamental characteristic of an ideal bureaucracy?

    A. Division of labor and specialization
    B. An established hierarchy
    C. Decentralization of authority
    D. A set of operating rules and regulations

17.____

18. As the number of subordinates in a manager's span of control increases, the actual number of possible relationships

    A. increases disproportionately to the number of subordinates
    B. increases in equal number to the number of subordinates
    C. reaches a stable level
    D. will first increase, then slowly decrease

18.____

19. Management experts generally believe that computer-based management information systems (MIS) have greater potential for improving the process of management than any other development in recent decades.
The one of the following which MOST accurately describes the objectives of MIS is to

   A. provide information for decision-making on planning, initiating, and controlling the operations of the various units of the organization
   B. establish mechanization of routine functions such as clerical records, payroll, inventory, and accounts receivable in order to promote economy and efficiency
   C. computerize decision-making on planning, initiating, organizing, and controlling the operations of an organization
   D. provide accurate facts and figures on the various programs of the organization to be used for purposes of planning and research

19._____

20. The one of the following which is the BEST application of the *management-by-exception* principle is that this principle

   A. stimulates communication and aids in management of crisis situations, thus reducing the frequency of decision-making
   B. saves time and reserves top management decisions only for crisis situations, thus reducing the frequency of decision-making
   C. stimulates communication, saves time, and reduces the frequency of decision-making
   D. is limited to crisis-management situations

20._____

21. Generally, each organization is dependent upon the availability of qualified personnel.
Of the following, the MOST important factor affecting the availability of qualified people to each organization is

   A. availability of public transportation
   B. the general rise in the educational levels of our population
   C. the rise of sentiment against racial discrimination
   D. pressure by organized community groups

21._____

22. A fundamental responsibility of all managers is to decide what physical facilities and equipment are needed to help attain basic goals.
Good planning for the purchase and use of equipment is seldom easy to do and is complicated most by the fact that

   A. organizations rarely have stable sources of supply
   B. nearly all managers tend to be better at personnel planning than at equipment planning
   C. decisions concerning physical resources are made too often on an emergency basis rather than under carefully prepared policies
   D. legal rulings relative to depreciation fluctuate very frequently

22._____

23. In attempting to reconcile managerial objectives and an individual employee's goals, it is generally LEAST desirable for management to

    A. recognize the capacity of the individual to contribute toward realization of managerial goals
    B. encourage self-development of the employee to exceed minimum job performance
    C. consider an individual employee's work separately from other employees
    D. demonstrate that an employee advances only to the extent that he contributes directly to the accomplishment of stated goals

24. As a management tool for discovering individual training needs, a job analysis would generally be of LEAST assistance in determining

    A. the performance requirements of individual jobs
    B. actual employee performance on the job
    C. acceptable standards of performance
    D. training needs for individual jobs

25. One of the major concerns of organizational managers today is how the spread of automation will affect them and the status of their positions. Realistically speaking, one can say that the MOST likely effect of our newer forms of highly automated technology on managers will be to

    A. make most top-level positions superfluous or obsolete
    B. reduce the importance of managerial work in general
    C. replace the work of managers with the work of technicians
    D. increase the importance of and demand for top managerial personnel

KEY (CORRECT ANSWERS)

1.	A	11.	B
2.	C	12.	A
3.	C	13.	B
4.	C	14.	D
5.	A	15.	D
6.	B	16.	C
7.	D	17.	C
8.	A	18.	A
9.	A	19.	A
10.	C	20.	C

21. B
22. C
23. C
24. B
25. D

SUPERVISION, ADMINISTRATION, MANAGEMENT, AND ORGANIZATION

EXAMINATION SECTION

TEST 1

DIRECTIONS: Each question or incomplete statement is followed by several suggested answers or completions. Select the one that BEST answers the question or completes the statement. *PRINT THE LETTER OF THE CORRECT ANSWER IN THE SPACE AT THE RIGHT.*

1. A supervisor scheduled and interview with a subordinate in order to discuss his unsatisfactory performance during the previous several weeks. The subordinate's work contained an excessive number of careless errors.
   After the interview, the supervisor, reviewing his own approach for self-examination, listed three techniques he had used in the interview, as follows:
   I. Specifically pointed out to the subordinate where he had failed to meet the standards expected.
   II. Shared the blame for certain management errors that had irritated the subordinate.
   III. Agreed with the subordinate on specific targets to be met during the period ahead.
   Of the following statements, the one that is MOST acceptable concerning the above three techniques is that
   A. all 3 techniques are correct
   B. techniques I and II are correct; III is not correct
   C. techniques II and III are correct; I is not correct
   D. techniques I and III are correct; II is not correct

2. Assume that the performance of an employee is not satisfactory.
   Of the following, the MOST effective way for a supervisor to attempt to improve the performance of the employee is to meet with him and to
   A. order him to change his behavior
   B. indicate the actions that are unsatisfactory and the penalties for them
   C. show him alternate ways of behaving and a method for him to evaluate his attempts at change
   D. suggest that he use the behavior of the supervisor as a model of acceptable conduct

3. Training employees to be productive workers is based on four fundamental principles:
   I. Demonstrate how the job should be done by telling and showing the correct operations step-by-step
   II. Allow the employee to get some of the feel of the job by allowing him to try it a bit
   III. Put him on the job while continuing to check his performance
   IV. Let him know why the job is important and why it must be done right

2 (#1)

The MOST logical order for these training steps is:
A. I, III, II, IV   B. I, IV, II, III   C. II, I, III, IV   D. IV, I, II, III

4. Sometimes a supervisor is faced with the need to train under-educated new employees.
The following five statements relate to training such employees.
I. Make the training general rather than specific
II. Rely upon demonstrations and illustrations whenever possible
III. Overtrain rather than undertrain by erring on the side of imparting a little more skill than is absolutely necessary
IV. Provide lots of follow-up on the job
V. Reassure and recognize frequently in order to increase self-confidence
Which of the following choices lists all the above statements that are generally CORRECT?
A. I, II, IV   B. II, III, IV, V   C. I, II, V   D. I, II, IV, V

4.____

5. One of the ways in which some supervisors train subordinates is to discuss the subordinate's weaknesses with them. Experts who have explored the actual feelings and reactions of subordinates in such situations have come to the conclusion that such interviews USUALLY
A. are seen by subordinates as a threat to their self-esteem
B. give subordinates a feeling of importance which leads to better learning
C. convince subordinates to accept the opinion of the supervisor
D. result in the development of better supervision

5.____

6. The one of the following which BEST describes the rate at which a trainee learns departmental procedures is that he *probably* will learn
A. at the same rate throughout if the material to be learned is complex
B. slowly in the beginning and then learning will accelerate steadily
C. quickly for a while, than slow down temporarily
D. at the same rate if the material to be learned is lengthy

6.____

7. Which of the following statements concerning the delegation of work to subordinate employees is generally CORRECT?
A. A supervisor's personal attitude toward delegation has a minimal effect on his skill in delegating.
B. A willingness to let subordinates make mistakes has a place in work delegation.
C. The element of trust has little impact on the effectiveness of work delegation.
D. The establishment of controls does not enhance the process of delegation.

7.____

8. Assume that you are the chairman of a group that has been formed to discuss and solve a particular problem. After a half-hour of discussion, you feel that the group is wandering off the point and is no longer discussing the problem.
In this situation, it would be BEST for you to
A. wait to see whether the group will get back on the track by itself
B. ask the group to stop and to try a different approach

8.____

C. ask the group to stop, decide where they are going, and then to decide how to continue
D. ask the group to stop, decide where they are going, and then to continue in a different direction

9. One method of group decision-making is the use of committees. Following are four statements concerning committees.
   I. Considering the value of each individual member's time, committees are costly.
   II. One result of committee decisions is that no one may be held responsible for the decision.
   III. Committees will make decisions more promptly than individuals.
   IV. Committee decisions tend to be balanced and to take different viewpoints into account.
   Which of the following choices lists all of the above statements that are generally CORRECT?
   A. I and II B. II and III C. I, II, IV D. II, III, IV

9.____

10. Assume that an employee bypasses his supervisor and comes directly to you, the superior officer, to ask for a short leave of absence because of a pressing personal problem. The employee did not first consult with his immediate supervisor because he believes that his supervisor is unfavorably biased against him.
    Of the following, the MOST desirable way for you to handle this situation is to
    A. instruct the employee that is it not appropriate for him to go over the head of his supervisor regardless of their personal relationship
    B. listen to a brief description of his problem and then tactfully suggest that he take the matter up with his supervisor before coming to you
    C. request that both the employee and his supervisor meet jointly with you in order to discuss the employee's problem and to get at the reasons behind their apparent difficulty
    D. listen carefully to the employee's problem and then, without committing yourself one way or the other, promise to discuss it with his supervisor

10.____

11. Which of the following statements concerning the motivation of subordinates is generally INCORRECT? The
    A. authoritarian approach as the method of supervision is likely to result in the setting of minimal performance standards for themselves by subordinates
    B. encouragement of competition among subordinates may lead to deterioration of teamwork
    C. granting of benefits by a supervisor to subordinates in order to gain their gratitude will result in maximum output by the subordinates
    D. opportunity to achieve job satisfaction has an important effect on motivating subordinates

11.____

12. Of the following, the MOST serious disadvantage of having a supervisor evaluate subordinates on the basis of measurable performance goals that are set jointly by the supervisor and the subordinates is that this results-oriented appraisal method
    A. focuses on past performance rather than plans for the future
    B. fails to provide sufficient feedback to help subordinates learn where they stand
    C. encourages the subordinates to conceal poor performance and set low goals
    D. changes the primary task of the supervisor from helping subordinates improve to criticizing their performance

13. A supervisor can BEST provide on-the-job satisfaction for his subordinates by
    A. providing rewards for good performance
    B. allowing them to decide when to do the assigned work
    C. motivating them to perform according to accepted procedures
    D. providing challenging work that achieves departmental objectives

14. Which of the following factors generally contributes MOST to job satisfaction among supervisory employees?
    A. Autonomy and independence on the job
    B. Job security
    C. Pleasant physical working conditions
    D. Adequate economic rewards

15. Large bureaucracies typically exhibit certain characteristics.
    Of the following, it would be CORRECT to state that such bureaucracies generally
    A. tend to oversimplify communications
    B. pay undue attention to informal organizations
    C. develop an attitude of "group-think" and conformity
    D. emphasize personal growth among employees

16. When positive methods fail to achieve conformity with accepted standards of conduct or performance, a negative type of action, punitive in nature, usually must follow.
    The one of the following that is usually considered LEAST important for the success of such punishment or negative discipline is that it be
    A. certain   B. swift   C. severe   D. consistent

17. Assume that you are a supervisor. Philip Smith, who is under your supervision, informs you that James Jones, who is also your subordinate, has been creating antagonism and friction within the unit because of his unnecessarily gruff manner in dealing with his co-workers. Smith's remarks confirm your own observations of Jones' behavior and its effects.

In handling this situation, the one of the following procedures which will probably be MOST effective is to
- A. ask Smith to act as an informal counselor to Jones and report the results to you
- B. counsel the other employees in your unit on methods of changing attitudes of people
- C. interview Jones and help him to understand this problem
- D. order Jones to carry out his responsibilities with greater consideration for the feelings of his co-workers

18. The principle relating to the number of subordinates who can be supervised effectively by one supervisor is COMMONLY known as   18.____
    - A. span of control
    - B. delegation of authority
    - C. optimum personnel assignment
    - D. organizational factor

19. Ascertaining and improving the level of morale in a public agency is one of the responsibilities of a conscientious supervisor.   19.____
    The one of the following aspects of subordinates' behavior which is NOT an indication of low morale is
    - A. lower-level employees participating in organizational decision-making
    - B. careless treatment of equipment
    - C. general deterioration of personal appearance
    - D. formation of cliques

20. Employees may resist changes in agency operations even though such changes are often necessary. If you, as a supervisor, are attempting to introduce a necessary change, you should first fully explain the reasons for it to your staff.   20.____
    Your NEXT step should be to
    - A. set specific goals and outline programs for all employees
    - B. invite employee participation in effectuating the change by asking for suggestions to accomplish it
    - C. discuss the need for improved work performance by city employees
    - D. point out the penalties for non-cooperation without singling out any employee by name

21. A supervisor should normally void giving orders in an offhand or casual manner MAINLY because his subordinates   21.____
    - A. are like most people and may resent being treated lightly
    - B. may attach little importance to these orders
    - C. may work best if given the choice of work methods
    - D. are unlikely to need instructions in most matters

22. Assume that, as a supervisor, you have just praised a subordinate. While he expresses satisfaction at your praise, he complains that it does not help him get promoted even though he is on a promotion eligible list, since there is no current vacancy.   22.____

In these circumstances, it would be BEST for you to
- A. minimize the importance of advancement and emphasize the satisfaction in the work itself
- B. follow up by pointing out some errors he has committed in the past
- C. admit that the situation exists, and express the hope that it will improve
- D. tell him that, until quite recently, advancement was even slower

23. Departmental policies are usually broad rules or guides for action. It is important for a supervisor to understand his role with respect to policy implementation.
Of the following, the MOST accurate description of this role is that a supervisor should
    - A. be apologetic toward his subordinates when applying unpopular policies to them
    - B. act within policy limits, although he can attempt to influence policy change by making his thoughts and observations known to his superior
    - C. arrange his activities so that he is able to deal simultaneously with situations that involve several policy matters
    - D. refrain as much as possible from exercising permissible discretion in applying policy to matters under his control

23.____

24. A supervisor should be aware that most subordinates will ask questions at meetings or group discussions in order to
    - A. stimulate other employees to express their opinions
    - B discover how they may be affected by the subjects under discussion
    - C. display their knowledge of the topics under discussion
    - D. consume time in order to avoid returning to their normal tasks

24.____

25. Don't assign responsibilities with conflicting objectives to the same work group. For example, to require a unit to monitor the quality of its own work is a bad practice.
This practice is MOST likely to be bad because
    - A. the chain of command will be unnecessarily lengthened
    - B. it is difficult to portray mixed duties accurately on an organization chart
    - C. employees may act in collusion to cover up poor work
    - D. the supervisor may delegate responsibilities which he should retain

25.____

KEY (CORRECT ANSWERS)

1. A
2. C
3. D
4. B
5. A

6. C
7. B
8. C
9. C
10. D

11. C
12. C
13. D
14. A
15. C

16. C
17. C
18. A
19. A
20. B

21. B
22. C
23. B
24. B
25. C

TEST 2

DIRECTIONS: Each question or incomplete statement is followed by several suggested answers or completions. Select the one that BEST answers the question or completes the statement. *PRINT THE LETTER OF THE CORRECT ANSWER IN THE SPACE AT THE RIGHT.*

1. Some supervisors use an approach in which each phase of the job is explained in broad terms supervision is general, and employees are allowed broad discretion in performing their job duties.
   Such a supervisory approach USUALLY affects employee motivation by
   A. improving morale and providing an incentive to work harder
   B. providing little or no incentive to work harder than the minimum required
   C. creating extra pressure, usually resulting in decreased performance
   D. reducing incentive to work and causing employees to feel neglected, particularly in performing complex tasks

   1.____

2. An employee complains to a superior officer that he has been treated unfairly by his supervisor, stating that other employees have been given less work to do and shown other forms of favoritism.
   Of the following, the BEST thing for the superior officer to do FIRST in order to handle this problem is to
   A. try to discover whether the subordinate has a valid complaint or if something else is the real problem
   B. ask other employees whether they feel their treatment is consistent and fair
   C. ask his supervisor to explain the charges
   D. see that the number of cases assigned to this employee is reduced

   2.____

3. Of the following, the MOST important condition needed to help a group of people to work well together and get the job done is
   A. higher salaries and a better working environment
   B. enough free time to relieve the tension
   C. good communication among everyone involved in the job
   D. assurance that everyone likes the work

   3.____

4. A supervisor realizes that a subordinate has called in sick for three Mondays out of the past four. These absences have interfered with staff performance and have been part of the cause of the unit's "behind schedule" condition.
   In order to correct this situation, it would be BEST for the supervisor to
   A. order the subordinate to explain his abuse of sick leave
   B. discuss with the subordinate the penalties for abusing sick leave
   C. discuss the matter with his own supervisor
   D. ask the subordinate in private whether he has a problem about coming to work

   4.____

5. Of the following, the MOST effective way for a supervisor to minimize undesirable rumors about new policies in the units under his supervision is to
   A. bypass the supervisor and communicate directly with the individual members of the units
   B. supply immediate and accurate information to everyone who is supposed to be informed
   C. play down the importance of the rumors
   D. issue all communications in written form

5.____

6. Which of the following is an indication that a superior officer is delegating authority PROPERLY?
   A. The superior officer closely checks the work of experienced subordinates at all stages in order to maintain standards.
   B. The superior officer gives overlapping assignments to insure that work is completed on time.
   C. The work of his subordinates can proceed and be completed during the superior officer's absence.
   D. The work of each supervisor is reviewed by him more than once in order to insure quality.

6.____

7. Of the following supervisory practices, the one which is MOST likely to foster employee morale is for the supervisor to
   A. take an active interest in subordinates' personal lives
   B. ignore mistakes
   C. give praise when justified
   D. permit rules to go unenforced occasionally

7.____

8. As the supervisor who is responsible for the implementation of new paperwork procedure, you note that the workers often do not follow the stipulated procedure.
   Before taking action, it would be ADVISABLE to realize that
   A. unconscious behavior, such as failure to adapt to change, is largely uncontrollable
   B. new procedures sometimes have to be modified and adapted after being tried out
   C. threats of disciplinary action will encourage approval of change
   D. procedures that fail should be abandoned and replaced

8.____

9. The one of the following which is generally considered to be the MOST significant criticism of the modern practice of effective human relations in management of large organizations is that human relations
   A. weakens management authority over employees
   B. gives employees control of operations
   C. can be used to manipulate and control employees
   D. weakens unions

9.____

10. Of the following, the MOST important reason why the supervisor should promote good supervisor-subordinate relations is to encourage his staff to
    A. feel important
    B. be more receptive to control
    C. be happy in their work
    D. meet production performance levels

11. A superior officer decides to assign a special report directly to an employee, bypassing his supervisor.
    In general, this practice is
    A. *advisable*, chiefly because it broadens the superior officer's span of authority
    B. *inadvisable*, chiefly because it undermines the authority of the supervisor in the eyes of his subordinates
    C. *advisable*, chiefly because it reduces the number of details the supervisor must know
    D. *inadvisable*, chiefly because it gives too much work to the employee

12. Many supervisors make it a practice to solicit suggestions from their subordinates and to encourage their participation in decision-making.
    The success of this type of supervision usually depends MOST directly upon the
    A. quality of leadership provided by the supervisor
    B. number of the supervisor's immediate subordinates
    C. availability of opportunities for employee advancement
    D. degree to which work assignments cause problems

13. Small informal groups or "cliques" often appear in a work setting.
    The one of the following which is generally an advantage of such groups, from an administrative point of view, is that they
    A. are not influenced by the administrative set-up of the office
    B. encourage socializing after working hours
    C. develop leadership roles among the office staff
    D. provide a "steam valve" for release of tension and fatigue

14. Assume that you are a superior officer in charge of several supervisors who, in turn, are in charge of a number of employees. The employees who are supervised by Jones (a supervisor) come as a group to you and indicate several reasons why Jones is incompetent and "has to go."
    Of the following, your BEST course of action to take FIRST is to
    A. direct the employees to see Jones about the matter
    B. suggest to the employees that they should attempt to work with Jones until he can be transferred
    C. discuss the possibility of terminating Jones with your superior
    D. ask Jones about the comments of the employees after they depart

4 (#2)

15. Of the following, the MAIN effect which the delegation of authority can have on the efficiency of an organization is to
    A. reduce the risk of decision-making errors
    B. produce uniformity of policy and action
    C. facilitate speedier decisions and actions
    D. enable closer control of operations

15.____

16. Of the following, the main DISADVANTAGE of temporarily transferring a newly appointed worker to another unit because of an unexpected vacancy is that the temporary nature of his assignment will, MOST likely,
    A. undermine his incentive to orient himself to his new job
    B. interfere with his opportunities for future advancement
    C. result in friction between himself and his new co-workers
    D. place his new supervisor in a difficult and awkward position

16.____

17. Assume that you, as a supervisor, have decided to raise the quality of work produced by your subordinates.
    The BEST of the following procedures for you to follow is to
    A. develop mathematically precise standards
    B. appoint a committee of subordinates to set firm and exacting guidelines, including penalties for deviations
    C. modify standards developed by supervisors in other organizations
    D. provide consistent evaluation of subordinates' work, furnishing training whenever advisable

17.____

18. Assume that a supervisor under your supervision strongly objects whenever changes are proposed which would improve the efficiency of his unit.
    Of the following, the MOST desirable way for you to change his attitude is to
    A. involve him in the planning and formulation of changes
    B. promise to recommend him for a more challenging assignment if he accepts changes
    C. threaten to have him transferred to another unit if he does not accept changes
    D. ask him to go along with the changes on a tentative, trial basis

18.____

19. Work goals may be defined in terms of units produced or in terms of standards of performance.
    Which of the following statements concerning work goals is CORRECT?
    A. Workers who have a share in establishing goals tend to set a fairly high standard for themselves, but fail to work toward it.
    B. Workers tend to produce according to what they believe are the goals actually expected of them.
    C. Since workers usually produce less than the established goals, management should set goals higher than necessary.
    D. The individual differences of workers can be minimized by using strict goals and invariable procedures.

19.____

20. Of the following, the type of employee who would respond BEST to verbal instructions given in the form of a suggestion or wish is the
    A. experienced worker who is eager to please
    B. sensitive and emotional worker
    C. hostile worker who is somewhat lazy
    D. slow and methodical worker

21. As a supervisor, you note that the output of an experienced staff member has dropped dramatically during the last two months. In addition, his error rate is significantly above that of other staff members. When you ask the employee the reason for his poor performance, he says, "Well, it's rather personal and I would rather not talk about it if you don't mind."
    At this point, which of the following would be the BEST reply?
    A. Tell him that you will give him two weeks to improve or you will discuss the matter with your own supervisor
    B. Insist that he tell you the reason for his poor work and assure him that anything personal will be kept confidential
    C. Say that you don't want to interfere, but, at the same time, his work has deteriorated, and that you're concerned about it
    D. Explain in a friendly manner that you are going to place a warning letter in his personnel folder that states he has one month in which to improve

22. Research studies have shown that employees who are strongly interested in achievement and advancement on the job usually want assignments where the chance of success is _____, and desire _____ supervisory evaluation of their performance.
    A. low; frequent
    B. high; general
    C. high; infrequent
    D. moderate; specific

23. Of the following, a function of the supervisor that concerns itself with the process of determining a course of action from alternatives is USUALLY referred to as
    A. decentralization
    B. planning
    C. controlling
    D. input

24. Favorable working conditions are an important variable in producing an effective work unit.
    Which of the following would be LEAST conducive in providing a favorable work situation?
    A. Applying a job enrichment program to a routine clerical position
    B. Setting practical goals for the work unit which are consistent with the overall objective of the agency
    C. Assigning individuals to positions which require a higher level of educational achievement than that which they possess
    D. Establishing a communications system which distributes information and provides feedback to all organizational levels

25. Ever supervisor within an organization should know to whom he reports and who reports to him.
Within the organization, this will MOST likely insure
   A. unity of command
   B. confidentiality of sensitive issues
   C. excellent morale
   D. the elimination of the grapevine

25._____

KEY (CORRECT ANSWERS)

1.	A	11.	B
2.	A	12.	A
3.	C	13.	D
4.	D	14.	D
5.	B	15.	C
6.	C	16.	A
7.	C	17.	D
8.	B	18.	A
9.	C	19.	B
10.	D	20.	A

21. C
22. D
23. B
24. C
25. A

TEST 3

DIRECTIONS: Each question or incomplete statement is followed by several suggested answers or completions. Select the one that BEST answers the question or completes the statement. *PRINT THE LETTER OF THE CORRECT ANSWER IN THE SPACE AT THE RIGHT.*

1. In trying to improve the motivation of his subordinates, a supervisor can achieve the BEST results by taking action based upon the assumption that *most* employees
    A. have an inherent dislike of work
    B. wish to be closely directed
    C. are more interested in security than in assuming responsibility
    D. will exercise self-direction without coercion

    1.____

2. Supervisors in public departments have many functions.
    Of the following, the function which is LEAST appropriate for a supervisor is to
    A. serve as a deputy for the administrator within his own unit
    B. determine needs within his unit and plan programs to meet these needs
    C. supervise, train, and evaluate all personnel assigned to his unit
    D. initiate and carry out fundraising projects, such as bazaars and carnivals, to buy needed equipment

    2.____

3. When there are conflicts or tensions between top management and lower-level employees in any public department, the supervisor should FIRSTS attempt to
    A. represent and enforce the management point of view
    B. act as the representative of the workers to get their ideas across to management
    C. serve as a two-way spokesman, trying to interpret each side to the other
    D. remain neutral, but keep informed of changes in the situation

    3.____

4. A probationary period for new employees is usually provided in public agencies.
    The MAJOR purpose of such a period is usually to
    A. allow a determination of employee's suitability for the position
    B. obtain evidence as to employee's ability to perform in a higher position
    C. conform to requirement that ethnic hiring goals be met for all positions
    D. train the new employee in the duties of the position

    4.____

5. An effective program of orientation for new employees usually includes all of the following EXCEPT
    A. having the supervisor introduce the new employee to his job, outlining his responsibilities and how to carry them out
    B. permitting the new worker to tour the facility or department, so he can observe all parts of it in action
    C. scheduling meetings for new employees, at which the job requirements are explained to them and they are given personnel manuals
    D. testing the new worker on his skills, and sending him to a centralized in-service workshop

    5.____

6. In-service training is an important responsibility of supervisors.
The MAJOR reason for such training is to
   A. avoid future grievance procedures, because employees might say they were not prepared to carry out their jobs
   B. maximize the effectiveness of the department by helping each employee perform at his full potential
   C. satisfy inspection teams from central headquarters of the department
   D. help prevent disagreements with members of the community

7. There are many forms of useful in-service training.
Of the following, the training method which is NOT an appropriate technique for leadership development is to
   A. provide special workshops or clinics in activity skills
   B. conduct pre-season institutes to familiarize new workers with the program of the department and with their roles
   C. schedule team meetings for problem-solving, including both supervisors and leaders
   D. have the leader rate himself on an evaluation form periodically

8. Of the following techniques of evaluating work training programs, the one that is BEST is to
   A. pass out a carefully designed questionnaire to the trainees at the completion of the program
   B. test the knowledge that trainees have both at the beginning of training and at its completion
   C. interview the trainees at the completion of the program
   D. evaluate performance before and after training for both a control group and an experimental group

9. Assume that a new supervisor is having difficulty making his instructions to subordinates clearly understood.
The one of the following which is the FIRST step he should take in dealing with this problem is to
   A. set up a training workshop in communication skills
   B. determine the extent and nature of the communication gap
   C. repeat both verbal and written instructions several times
   D. simplify his written and spoken vocabulary

10. Discipline of employees is usually a supervisor's responsibility. There may be several useful forms of disciplinary action in public employment.
Of the following, the form that is LEAST appropriate is the
    A. written reprimand or warning
    B. involuntary transfer to another work setting
    C. demotion or suspension
    D. assignment of added hours of work each week

11. Of the following, the MOST effective means of dealing with employee disciplinary problems is to
    A. give personality tests to individuals to identify their psychological problems
    B. distribute and discuss a policy manual containing exact rules governing employee behavior
    C. establish a single, clear penalty to be imposed for all wrongdoing irrespective of degree
    D. have supervisors get to know employees well through social mingling

12. A recently developed technique for appraising work performance is to have the supervisor record on a continual basis all significant incidents in each subordinate's behavior that indicate unsuccessful action and those that indicate poor behavior.
    Of the following, a major DISADVANTAGE of this method of performance appraisal is that it
    A. often leads to overly close supervision
    B. results in competition among those subordinates being evaluated
    C. tends to result in superficial judgments
    D. lacks objectivity for evaluating performance

13. Assume that you are a supervisor and have observed the performance of an employee during a period of time. You have concluded that his performance needs improvement.
    In order to approve his performance, it would, therefore, be BEST for you to
    A. note your findings in the employee's personnel folder so that his behavior is a matter of record
    B. report the findings to the personnel officer so he can take prompt action
    C. schedule a problem-solving conference with the employee
    D. recommend his transfer to simpler duties

14. When an employee's absences or latenesses seem to be nearing excessiveness, the supervisor should speak with him to find out what the problem is.
    Of the following, if such a discussion produces no reasonable explanation, the discussion usually BEST serves to
    A. affirm clearly the supervisor's adherence to proper policy
    B. alert other employees that such behavior is unacceptable
    C. demonstrate that the supervisor truly represents higher management
    D. notify the employee that his behavior is being observed and evaluated

15. Assume that an employee willfully and recklessly violates an important agency regulation. The nature of the violation is of such magnitude that it demands immediate action, but the facts of the case are not entirely clear. Further assume that the supervisor is free to make any of the following recommendations.

The MOST appropriate action for the supervisor to take is to recommend that the employee be
A. discharged   B. suspended   C. forced to resign   D. transferred

16. Although employees' titles may be identical, each position in that title may be considerably different.
Of the following, a supervisor should carefully assign each employee to a specific position based PRIMARILY on the employee's
A. capability   B. experience   C. education   D. seniority

17. The one of the following situations where it is MOST appropriate to transfer an employee to a *similar* assignment is one in which the employee
A. lacks motivation and interest
B. experiences a personality conflict with his supervisor
C. is negligent in the performance of his duties
D. lacks capacity or ability to perform assigned tasks

18. The one of the following which is LEAST likely to be affected by improvement in the morale of personnel is employee
A. skill   B. absenteeism   C. turnover   D. job satisfaction

19. The one of the following situations in which it is LEAST appropriate for a supervisor to delegate authority to subordinates is where the supervisor
A. lacks confidence in his own abilities to perform certain work
B. is overburdened and cannot handle all his responsibilities
C. refers all disciplinary problems to his subordinate
D. has to deal with an emergency or crisis

20. Of the following, the BEST attitude toward the use of volunteers in programs is that volunteers should be
A. discouraged, since they cannot be depended upon to show up regularly
B. employed as a last resort when paid personnel are unavailable
C. seen as an appropriate means of providing leadership, when effectively recruited and supervised
D. eliminated to raise the professionalism of personnel

21. A supervisor finds that he is spending too much time on routine tasks, and not enough time on coordinating the work of his employees.
It would be MOST advisable for this supervisor to
A. delegate the task of work coordination to a capable subordinate
B. eliminate some of the routine tasks that the unit is required to perform
C. assign some of the routine tasks to his subordinates
D. postpone the performance of routine tasks until he has achieved proper coordination of his employees' work

22. Of the following, the MOST important reason for having an office manual in looseleaf form rather than in permanent binding is that the looseleaf form
    A. facilitates the addition of new material and the removal of obsolete material
    B. permits several people to use different sections of the manual at the same time
    C. is less expensive to prepare than permanent binding
    D. is more durable than permanent binding

23. In his first discussion with a newly appointed employee, the LEAST important of the following topics for a supervisor of a unit to include is the
    A. duties the subordinate is expected to perform on the job
    B. functions of the unit
    C. methods of determining standards of performance
    D. nature and duration of the training the subordinate will receive on the job

24. A supervisor has just been told by a subordinate, Mr. Jones, that another employee, Mr. Smith, deliberately disobeyed an important rule of the department by taking home some confidential departmental material.
    Of the following courses of action, it would be MOST advisable for the supervisor FIRST to
    A. discuss the matter privately, with both Mr. Jones and Mr. Smith at the same time
    B. call a meeting of the entire staff and discuss the matter generally without mentioning any employee by name
    C. arrange to supervise Mr. Smith's activities more closely
    D. discuss the matter privately with Mr. Smith

25. The one of the following actions which would be MOST efficient and economical for a supervisor to take to minimize the effect of seasonal fluctuations in the workload of his unit is to
    A. increase his permanent staff until it is large enough to handle the work of the busy season
    B. request the purchase of time and labor-saving equipment to be used primarily during the busy season
    C. lower, temporarily, the standards for quality of work performance during peak loads
    D. schedule for the slow season work that it is not essential to perform during the busy season

KEY (CORRECT ANSWERS)

1. D
2. D
3. C
4. A
5. D

6. B
7. D
8. D
9. B
10. D

11. B
12. A
13. C
14. D
15. B

16. A
17. B
18. A
19. C
20. C

21. C
22. A
23. C
24. D
25. D

TEST 4

DIRECTIONS: Each question or incomplete statement is followed by several suggested answers or completions. Select the one that BEST answers the question or completes the statement. *PRINT THE LETTER OF THE CORRECT ANSWER IN THE SPACE AT THE RIGHT.*

1. Assume that, while instructing a worker on a new procedure, the instructor asks, at frequent intervals, whether there are any questions.
   His asking for questions is a
   A. *good practice*, because it affords the worker an opportunity to participate actively in the lesson
   B. *good practice*, because it may reveal points that are not understood by the worker
   C. *poor practice*, because workers generally find it embarrassing to ask questions
   D. *poor practice*, because it may result in wasting time on irrelevant matters

    1.____

2. Any person thoroughly familiar with the specific steps in a particular type of work is well-qualified to serve as a training course instructor in the work.
   This statement is *erroneous* CHIEFLY because
   A. a qualified instructor cannot be expected to have detailed information about many specific fields
   B. a person who knows a field thoroughly may not be good at passing his knowledge along to others
   C. it is practically impossible for any instructor to be acquainted with all the specific steps in a particular type of work
   D. what is true of one type of work is not necessarily true of other types of work

    2.____

3. Of the following traits, the one that is LEAST essential for the "ideal" supervisor is that she
   A. be consistent in her interpretation of the rules and policies of the agency for which she works
   B. is able to judge a person's ability at her first meeting with that person
   C. know her own job thoroughly
   D. appreciate and acknowledge honest effort and above-average work

    3.____

4. The one of the following which is generally the basic reason for using standard procedure is to
   A. serve as a basis for formulating policies
   B. provide the sequence of steps for handling recurring activities
   C. train new employees in the policies and objectives
   D. facilitate periodic review of standard practices

    4.____

5. An employee, while working at the bookkeeping machine, accidentally kicks off the holdup alarm system. She notifies the supervisor that she can hear the holdup alarm bell ringing, and requests that the holdup alarm system be reset. After the holdup alarm system has been reset, the supervisor should notify the manager that the alarm
   A. is in proper working order
   B. should be shut off while the employee is working the bookkeeping machine to avoid another such accident
   C. kick-plate should be moved away from the worker's reception window so that it cannot be set off accidentally
   D. should be relocated so that it cannot be heard in the bookkeeping office

5.____

6. A supervisor who spends a considerate amount of time correcting subordinates' procedural errors should consider FIRST the possibility of
   A. disciplining those who make errors consistently
   B. instituting refresher training sessions
   C. redesigning work forms
   D. requesting that the requirements for entry-level jobs be changed

6.____

7. A supervisor has a subordinate who has been late the past four mornings. Of the following, the MOST important action for the supervisor to take FIRST is to
   A. read the rules concerning lateness to the employee in an authoritative manner
   B. give the subordinate a chance to explain the reason for his lateness
   C. tell the employee he must come in on time the next day
   D. ask the friends of the employee whether they can tell him the reason for the employee's lateness

7.____

8. During a conversation, a subordinate tells his supervisor about a family problem For the supervisor to give EXPLICIT advice to the subordinate would be
   A. *desirable*, primarily because a happy employee is more likely to be productive
   B. *undesirable*, primarily because the supervisor should not allow a subordinate to discuss personal problems
   C. *desirable*, primarily because their personal relations will show a marked improvement
   D. *undesirable*, primarily because a supervisor should not take responsibility for handling a subordinate's personal problem

8.____

9. As a supervisor, you have received instructions for a drastic change in the procedure for processing cases.
   Of the following, the approach which is MOST likely to result in acceptance of the change by your subordinates is for you to
   A. inform all subordinates of the change by written memo so that they will have guidelines to follow
   B. ask your superior to inform the unit members about the change at a staff meeting

9.____

C. recruit the most experienced employee in the unit to give individual instruction to the other unit members
D. discuss the change and the reasons for it with the staff so that they understand their role in its implementation

10. Of the following, the principle which should GENERALLY guide a supervisor in the training of employees under his supervision is that
    A. training of employees should be delegated to more experienced employees in the same title
    B. primary emphasis should be placed on training for future assignments
    C. the training process should be a highly individual matter
    D. training efforts should concentrate on employees who have the greatest potential

10.____

KEY (CORRECT ANSWERS)

1.	B	6.	B
2.	B	7.	B
3.	B	8.	D
4.	B	9.	D
5.	D	10.	C

SUPERVISION, ADMINISTRATION, MANAGEMENT AND ORGANIZATION
EXAMINATION SECTION
TEST 1

DIRECTIONS: Each question or incomplete statement is followed by several suggested answers or completions. Select the one that BEST answers the question or completes the statement. *PRINT THE LETTER OF THE CORRECT ANSWER IN THE SPACE AT THE RIGHT.*

1. The one of the following practices by a supervisor which is MOST likely to lead to confusion and inefficiency is for him to
   A. give orders verbally directly to the man assigned to the job
   B. issue orders only in writing
   C. follow up his orders after issuing them
   D. relay his orders to the men through co-workers

1.____

2. If you are given an oral order by a supervisor which you do not understand completely, you should
   A. use your own judgment
   B. discuss the order with your men
   C. ask your supervisor for a further explanation
   D. carry out that part of the order which you do understand and then ask for more information

2.____

3. An orientation program for a group of new employees should NOT ordinarily include a
   A. review of the organizational structure of the agency
   B. detailed description of the duties of each new employee
   C. description of the physical layout of the repair shop
   D. statement of the rules pertaining to sick leave, vacation, and holidays

3.____

4. The MOST important rule to follow with regard to discipline is that a man should be disciplined
   A. after everyone has had time to "cool off"
   B. as soon as possible after the infraction of rules
   C. only for serious rule violations
   D. before he makes a mistake

4.____

5. If the men under your supervision continue to work effectively even when you are out sick for several days, it would MOST probably indicate that
   A. the men are merely trying to show you up
   B. the men are in constant fear of you and are glad you are away
   C. you have trained your men properly and have their full cooperation
   D. you are serving no useful purpose since the men can get along without you

5.____

6. When evaluating subordinates, the employee who should be rated HIGHEST by his supervisor is the one who
   A. never lets the supervisor do heavy lifting
   B. asks many questions about the work
   C. makes many suggestions on work procedures
   D. listens to instructions and carries them out

   6.____

7. Of the following, the factor which is generally MOST important to the conduct of successful training is
   A. time   B. preparation   C. equipment   D. space

   7.____

8. One of the MAJOR disadvantages of "on-the-job" training is that it
   A. requires a long training period for instructors
   B. may not be progressive
   C. requires additional equipment
   D. may result in the waste of supplies

   8.____

9. For a supervisor to train workers in several trades which involve various skills, presents many training problems.
   The one of the following which is NOT true in such a training situation is that
   A. less supervision is required
   B. greater planning for training is required
   C. rotation of assignments is necessary
   D. less productivity can be expected

   9.____

10. For a supervisor of repair workers to have each worker specialize in learning a single trade is GENERALLY
    A. *desirable*; each worker will become expert in his assigned trade
    B. *undesirable*; there is less flexibility of assignments possible when each worker has learned only a single trade
    C. *desirable*; the training responsibility of the supervisor is simplified when each worker is required to learn a single trade
    D. *undesirable*; workers lose interest quickly when they know they are expected to learn a single trade

    10.____

11. An IMPORTANT advantage of standardizing work procedures is that it
    A. develops all-around skills
    B. makes the work less monotonous
    C. provides an incentive for good work
    D. enable the work to be done with less supervision

    11.____

12. Generally, the GREATEST difficulty in introducing new work methods is due to the fact that
    A. men become set in their ways
    B. the old way is generally better
    C. only the department will benefit from changes
    D. explaining new methods is time consuming

    12.____

13. Assume that you are required to transmit an order with, which you do not agree, to your subordinates.
    In this case, it would be BEST for you to
    A. ask one of your superiors to transmit the order
    B. refuse to transmit an order with which you do not agree
    C. transmit the order but be sure to explain that you do not agree with it
    D. transmit the order and enforce it to the best of your ability

14. The MAIN reason for written orders is that
    A. proper blame can be placed if the order is not carried out
    B. the order will be carried out faster
    C. the order can be properly analyzed as to its meaning
    D. there will be no doubt as to what the order says

15. You have been informed unofficially by another shop manager that some of the men under your supervision are loafing on the job.
    This situation can be BEST handled by
    A. telling the man to mind his own business
    B. calling the men together and reprimanding them
    C. having the men work under your direct supervision
    D. arranging to make spot checks at more frequent intervals

16. Suggestions on improving methods of doing work, when submitted by a new employee, should be
    A. examined for possible merit because the new man may have a fresh viewpoint
    B. ignored because it would make the old employees resentful
    C. disregarded because he is too unfamiliar with the work
    D. examined only for the purpose of judging the new man

17. One of your employees often slows down the work of his crew by playing practical jokes.
    The BEST way to handle this situation is to
    A. arrange for his assignment to more than his share of unpleasant jobs
    B. warn him that he must stop this practice at once
    C. ignore this situation for he will soon tire of it
    D. ask your supervisor to transfer him

18. One of your men is always complaining about working conditions, equipment, and his fellow workers.
    The BEST action for you to take in this situation is to
    A. have this man work alone if possible
    B. consider each complaint on is merits
    C. tell him bluntly that you will not listen to any of his complaints
    D. give this man the worst jobs until he quits complaining

19. It is generally agreed that men who are interested in their work will do the best work.
    A supervisor can LEAST stimulate this interest by
    A. complimenting men on good work
    B. correcting men on their working procedures
    C. striving to create overtime for his men
    D. recommending merit raises for excellent work

20. If you, as a supervisor, have criticized one of your men for making a mistake, you should
    A. remind the man of his error from time to time to keep him on his toes
    B. overlook any further errors which this man may make, otherwise he may feel he is a victim of discrimination
    C. give the man the opportunity to redeem himself
    D. impress the man with the fact that all his work will be closely checked from then on

21. In his efforts to maintain standards of performance, a shop manager uses a system of close supervision to detect or catch errors.
    An *opposite* method of accomplishing the *same* objective is to employ a program which
    A. instills in each employee a pride of workmanship to do the job correctly the first time
    B. groups each job accordingly to the importance to the overall objectives of the program
    C. makes the control of quality the responsibility of an inspector
    D. emphasizes that there is a "one" best way for an employee to do s specific job

22. Assume that after taking over a repair shop, a shop manager feels that he is taking too much time maintaining records.
    He should
    A. temporarily assign this job to one of his senior repair crew chiefs
    B. get together with his supervisor to determine if all these records are needed
    C. stop keeping those records which he believes are unnecessary
    D. spend a few additional hours each day until his records are current

23. In order to apply performance standards to employees engaged in repair shop activities, a shop manager must FIRST
    A. allow workers to decide for themselves the way to do the job
    B. determine what is acceptable as satisfactory work
    C. separate the more difficult tasks from the simpler tasks
    D. stick to an established work schedule

24. Of the following actions a shop manager can take to determine whether the vehicles used in his shop are being utilized properly, the one which will give him the LEAST meaningful information is
    A. conducting an analysis of vehicle assignments
    B. reviewing the number of miles traveled by each vehicle with and without loads
    C. recording the unloaded weights of each vehicle
    D. comparing the amount of time vehicles are parked at job sites with the time required to travel to and from job sites

25. For a shop manager, the MOST important reason that equipment which is used infrequently should be considered for disposal is that
    A. the time required for its maintenance could be better used elsewhere
    B. such equipment may cause higher management to think that your shop is not busy
    C. the men may resent having to work on such equipment
    D. such equipment usually has a higher breakdown rate in operation

KEY (CORRECT ANSWERS)

1.	D	11.	D
2.	C	12.	A
3.	B	13.	D
4.	B	14.	D
5.	C	15.	D
6.	D	16.	A
7.	B	17.	B
8.	B	18.	B
9.	A	19.	C
10.	B	20.	C

21.	A
22.	B
23.	B
24.	C
25.	A

TEST 2

DIRECTIONS: Each question or incomplete statement is followed by several suggested answers or completions. Select the one that BEST answers the question or completes the statement. *PRINT THE LETTER OF THE CORRECT ANSWER IN THE SPACE AT THE RIGHT.*

1. Assume that one of your subordinates approaches you with a grievance concerning working conditions.
   Of the following, the BEST action for you to take first is to
   A. "soft-soap" him, since most grievances are imaginary
   B. settle the grievance to his satisfaction
   C. try to talk him out of his complaint
   D. listen patiently and sincerely to the complaint

1.____

2. Of the following, the BEST way for a supervisor to help a subordinate learn a new skill which requires the use of tools is for him to give this subordinate
   A. a list of good books on the subject
   B. lectures on the theoretical aspects of the task
   C. opportunities to watch someone using the tools
   D. opportunities to practice the skill, under close supervision

2.____

3. A supervisor finds that his own work load is excessive because several of his subordinates are unable to complete their assignments.
   Of the following, the BEST action for him to take to improve this situation is to
   A. discipline these subordinates
   B. work overtime
   C. request additional staff
   D. train these subordinates in more efficient work methods

3.____

4. The one of the following situations which is MOST likely to be the result of *poor* morale is a(n)
   A. high rate of turnover
   B. decrease in number of requests by subordinates for transfers
   C. increase in the backlog of work
   D. decrease in the rate of absenteeism

4.____

5. As a supervisor, you find that several of your subordinates are not meeting their deadlines because they are doing work assigned to them by one of your fellow supervisors without your knowledge.
   Of the following, the BEST course of action for you to take in this situation is to
   A. tell the other supervisors to make future assignments through you
   B. assert your authority by publicly telling the other supervisors to stop issuing orders to your workers
   C. go along with this practice; it is an effective way to fully utilize the available manpower
   D. take the matter directly to your immediate supervisor without delay

5.____

6. If a supervisor of a duplicating section in an agency hears a rumor concerning a change in agency personnel policy through the "grapevine," he should
   A. *repeat* it to his subordinates so they will be informed
   B. *not repeat* it to his subordinates before he determines the facts because, as supervisor, his work may give it unwarranted authority
   C. *repeat* it to his subordinates so that they will like him for confiding in them
   D. *not repeat* it to his subordinates before he determines the facts because a duplicating section is not concerned with matters of policy

6.____

7. When teaching a new employee how to operate a machine, a supervisor should FIRST
   A. let the employee try to operate the machine by himself, since he can learn only by his mistakes
   B. explain the process to him with the use of diagrams before showing him the machine
   C. have him memorize the details of the operation from the manual
   D. explain and demonstrate the various steps in the process, making sure he understands each step

7.____

8. If a subordinate accuses you of always giving him the least desirable assignments, you should IMMEDIATELY
   A. tell him that it is not true and you do not want to hear any more about it
   B. try to get specific details from him, so that you can find out what his impressions are based on
   C. tell him that you distribute assignments in the fairest way possible and he must be mistaken
   D. ask him what current assignment he has that he does not like, and assign it to someone else

8.____

9. Suppose that the production of an operator under your supervision has been unsatisfactory and you have decided to have a talk with him about it.
   During the interview, it would be BEST for you to
   A. discuss only the subordinate's weak points so that he can overcome them
   B. discuss only the subordinate's strong points so that he will not become discouraged
   C. compare the subordinate's work with that of his co-workers so that he will know what is expected of him
   D. discuss both his weak and strong points so that he will get a view of his overall performance

9.____

10. Suppose that an operator under your supervision makes a mistake in color on a 2,000-page job and runs it on white paper instead of on blue paper.
    Of the following, your BEST course in these circumstances would be to point out the error to the operator and
    A. have the operator rerun the job immediately on blue paper
    B. send the job to the person who ordered it without comment
    C. send the job to the person who ordered it and tell him it could not be done on blue paper
    D. ask the person who ordered the job whether the white paper is acceptable

10.____

11. Assuming that all your subordinates have equal technical competence, the BEST policy for a supervisor to follow when making assignments of undesirable jobs would be to
    A. distribute them as evenly as possible among his subordinates
    B. give them to the subordinate with the poorest attendance record
    C. ask the subordinate with the least seniority to do them
    D. assign them to the subordinate who is least likely to complain

11.____

12. To get the BEST results when training a number of subordinates at the same time, a supervisor should
    A. treat all of them in an identical manner to avoid accusations of favoritism
    B. treat them all fairly, but use different approaches in dealing with people of different personality types
    C. train only one subordinate, and have him train the others, because this will save a lot of the supervisor's time
    D. train first the subordinates who learn quickly so as to make the others think that the operation is easy to learn

12.____

13. Assume that, after a week's vacation, you return to find that one of your subordinates has produced a job which is unsatisfactory.
    Your BEST course of action at that time would be to
    A. talk to your personnel department about implementing disciplinary action
    B. discuss unsatisfactory work in the unit at a meeting with all of your subordinates
    C. discuss the job with the subordinate to determine why he was unable to do it properly
    D. ignore the matter, because it is too late to correct the mistake

13.____

14. Suppose that an operator under your supervision informs you that Mr. Y, a senior administrator in your agency, has been submitting for copying many papers which are obviously personal in nature. The operator wants to know what to do about it, since the duplication of personal papers is against agency rules.
    Your BEST course of action in these circumstances would be to
    A. tell the operator to pretend not to notice the content of the material and continue to copy whatever is given to him
    B. tell the operator that Mr. Y, as a senior administrator, must have gotten special permission to have personal papers duplicated
    C. have the operator refer Mr. Y to you and inform Mr. Y yourself that duplication of personal papers is against agency rules
    D. call Mr. Y's superior and tell him that Mr. Y has been having personal papers duplicated, which is against agency rules

14.____

15. Assume that you are teaching a certain process to an operator under your supervision.
    In order to BEST determine whether he is actually learning what you are teaching, you should ask questions which
    A. can easily be answered by a "yes" or "no"
    B. require or encourage guessing

15.____

C. require a short description of what has been taught
D. are somewhat ambiguous so as to make the learner think about the procedures in question

16. If an employee is chronically late or absent, as his supervisor, it would be BEST for you to
    A. let his work pile up so he can see that no one else will do it for him
    B. discuss the matter with him and stress the importance of finding a solution
    C. threaten to enter a written report on the matter into his personnel file
    D. work out a system with him so he can have a different work schedule than the other employees

16.____

17. Assume that you have a subordinate who has just finished a basic training course in the operation of a machine.
    Giving him a large and difficult FIRST assignment would be
    A. *good*, because it would force him to "learn the ropes"
    B. *bad*, because he would probably have difficulty in carrying it out, discouraging him and resulting in a waste of time and supplies
    C. *good*, because how he handles it would give you an excellent basis for judging his competence
    D. *bad*, because he would probably assume that you are discriminating against him

17.____

18. After putting a new employee under your supervision through an initial training period, assigning him to work with a more experienced employee for a while would be a
    A. *good* idea, because it would give him the opportunity to observe what he had been taught and to participate in production himself
    B. *bad* idea, because he should not be required to work under the direction of anyone who is not his supervisor
    C. *good* idea, because it would raise the morale of the more experienced employee who could use him to do all the unpleasant chores
    D. *bad* idea, because the best way for him to learn would be to give him full responsibility for assignments right away

18.____

19. Assume that a supervisor is responsible for ordering supplies for the duplicating section in his agency.
    Which one of the following actions would be MOST helpful in determining when to place orders so that an adequate supply of materials will be on hand at all times?
    A. Taking an inventory of supplies on hand at least every two months
    B. Asking his subordinates to inform him when they see that supplies are low
    C. Checking the inventory of supplies whenever he has time
    D. Keeping a running inventory of supplies and a record of estimated needs

19.____

5 (#2)

20. Routine procedures that have worked well in the past should be reviewed periodically by a supervisor MAINLY because
    A. they may have become outdated or in need of revision
    B. employees might dislike the procedures even though they have proven successful in the past
    C. these reviews are the main part of a supervisor's job
    D. this practice serves to give the supervisor an idea of how productive his subordinates are

20.____

21. Assume that an employee tells his supervisor about a grievance he has against a co-worker. The supervisor assures the employee that he will immediately take action to eliminate the grievance.
    The supervisor's attitude should be considered
    A. *correct*, because a good supervisor is one who can come to a quick decision
    B. *incorrect*, because the supervisor should have told the employee that he will investigate the grievance and then determine a future course of action
    C. *correct*, because the employee's morale will be higher, resulting in greater productivity
    D. *incorrect*, because the supervisor should remain uninvolved and let the employees settle grievances between themselves

21.____

22. If an employee's work output is low and of poor quality due to faulty work habits, the MOST constructive of the following ways for a supervisor to correct this situation generally is to
    A. discipline the employee
    B. transfer the employee to another unit
    C. provide additional training
    D. check the employee's work continuously

22.____

23. Assume that it becomes necessary for a supervisor to ask his staff to work overtime.
    Which one of the following techniques is MOST likely to win their willing cooperation to do this?
    A. Explain that this is part of their job specification entitled, "performs related work"
    B. Explain the reason it is necessary for the employees to work overtime
    C. Promise the employees special consideration regarding future leave matters
    D. Explain that if the employees do not work overtime, they will face possible disciplinary action

23.____

24. If an employee's work performance has recently fallen below established minimum standards for quality and quantity, the threat of demotion or other disciplinary measures as an attempt to improve this employee's performance would probably be the MOST acceptable and effective course of action
    A. *only* after other more constructive measures have failed
    B. *if* applied uniformly to all employees as soon as performance falls below standard

24.____

25. If, as a supervisor, it becomes necessary for you to assign an employee to supervise your unit during your vacation, it would generally be BEST to select the employee who
    A. is the best technician on the staff
    B. can get the work out smoothly, without friction
    C. has the most seniority
    D. is the most popular with the group

25._____

KEY (CORRECT ANSWERS)

1. D
2. D
3. D
4. A
5. A

6. B
7. D
8. B
9. D
10. D

11. A
12. B
13. C
14. C
15. C

16. B
17. B
18. A
19. D
20. A

21. B
22. C
23. B
24. A
25. B

TEST 3

DIRECTIONS: Each question or incomplete statement is followed by several suggested answers or completions. Select the one that BEST answers the question or completes the statement. *PRINT THE LETTER OF THE CORRECT ANSWER IN THE SPACE AT THE RIGHT.*

1. An employee under your supervision has demonstrated a deep-seated personality problem that has begun to affect his work.
   This situation should be
   A. *ignored*, mainly because such problems usually resolve themselves
   B. *handled*, mainly because the employee should be assisted in seeking professional help
   C. *ignored*, mainly because the employee will consider any advice as interference
   D. *handled*, mainly because the supervisors should be qualified to resolve deep-seated personality problems

    1.____

2. Of the following, a supervisor will usually be MOST successful in maintaining employee morale while providing effective leadership if he
   A. takes prompt disciplinary action every time it is needed
   B. gives difficult assignments only to those workers who ask for such work
   C. promises his workers anything reasonable they request
   D. relies entirely on his staff for decisions

    2.____

3. When a supervisor makes an assignment to his subordinates, he should include a clear statement of what results are expected when the assignment is completed.
   Of the following, the BEST reason for following this procedure is that it will
   A. make it unnecessary for the supervisor to check on the progress of the work
   B. stimulate initiative and cooperation on the part of the more responsible workers
   C. give the subordinates a way to judge whether their work is meeting the requirements
   D. give the subordinates the feeling that they have some freedom of action

    3.____

4. Assume that, on a new employee's first day of work, his supervisor gives him a good orientation by telling him the general regulations and procedures used in the office and introducing him to his department head and fellow employees.
   For the remainder of the day, it would be BEST for the supervisor to
   A. give him steady instruction in all phases of his job, while stressing its most important aspects
   B. have him observe a fellow employee perform the duties of the job
   C. instruct him in that part of the job which he would prefer to learn first
   D. give him a simple task which requires little instruction and allows him to familiarize himself with the surroundings

    4.____

5. When it becomes necessary to criticize subordinates because several errors in the unit's work have been discovered, the supervisor should USUALLY
   A. focus on the job operation and avoid placing personal blame
   B. make every effort to fix blame and admonish the person responsible
   C. include in the criticism those employees who recognize and rectify their own mistakes
   D. repeat the criticism at regular intervals in order to impress the subordinates with the seriousness of their errors

5.____

6. If two employees under your supervision are continually bickering and cannot get along together, the FIRST action that you should take is to
   A. investigate possible ways of separating them
   B. ask your immediate superior for the procedure to follow in this situation
   C. determine the cause of their difficulty
   D. develop a plan and tell both parties to try it

6.____

7. In general, it is appropriate to recommend the transfer of an employee for all of the following reasons EXCEPT
   A. rewarding him
   B. providing him with a more challenging job
   C. remedying an error in initial placement
   D. disciplining him

7.____

8. Of the following, the MAIN disadvantage of basing a training and development program on a series of lectures is that the lecture technique
   A. does not sufficiently involve trainees in the learning process
   B. is more costly than other methods of training
   C. cannot be used to facilitate the understanding of difficult information
   D. is time consuming and inefficient

8.____

9. A supervisor has been assigned to train a new employee who is properly motivated but has made many mistakes.
   In the interview between the supervisor and employee about this problem, the employee should FIRST be
   A. asked if he can think of anything that he can do to improve his work
   B. complimented sincerely on some aspect of his work that is satisfactory
   C. asked to explain why he made the mistake
   D. advised that he may be dismissed if he continues to be careless

9.____

10. In training subordinates for more complex work, a supervisor must be aware of the progress that the subordinates are making.
    Determination of the results that have been accomplished by training is a concept commonly known as
    A. reinforcement   B. feedback
    C. cognitive dissonance   D. the halo effect

10.____

11. Assume that one of your subordinates loses interest in his work because he feels that your recent evaluation of his performance was unfair.
    The one of the following which is the BEST way to help him is to
    A. establish frequent deadlines for his work
    B. discuss his feelings and attitude with him
    C. discuss with him only the positive aspects of his performance
    D. arrange for his transfer to another unit

12. Informal organizations often develop at work.
    Of the following, the supervisor should realize that these groups will USUALLY
    A. determine work pace through unofficial agreements
    B. restrict vital communication channels
    C. lower morale by providing a chance to spread grievances
    D. provide leaders who will substitute for the supervisor when he is absent

13. Assume that you, the supervisor, have called to your office a subordinate whom, on several recent occasions, you have seen using the office telephone for personal use.
    In this situation, it would be MOST appropriate to begin the interview by
    A. discussing the disciplinary action that you believe to be warranted
    B. asking the subordinate to explain the reason for his personal use of the office telephone
    C. telling the subordinate about other employees who were disciplined for the same offense
    D. informing the subordinate that he is not to use the office telephone under any circumstances until further notice

14. Of the following, the success of any formal training program depends PRIMARILY upon the
    A. efficient and thorough preparation of materials, facilities, and procedures for instruction
    B. training program's practical relevance to the on-the-job situation
    C. scheduling of training sessions so as to minimize interference with normal job responsibilities
    D. creation of a positive initial reception on the part of the trainees

15. All of the following are legitimate purposes for regularly evaluating employee performance EXCEPT
    A. stimulating improvement in performance
    B. developing more accurate standards to be used in future ratings
    C. encouraging a spirit of competition
    D. allowing the employee to set realistic work goals for himself

16. A certain supervisor is very conscientious. He wants to receive personally all reports, correspondence, etc., and to be completely involved in all of the unit's operations. However, he is having difficulty in keeping up with the growing amount of paperwork.

4 (#3)

Of the following, the MOST desirable course of action for him to take is to
- A. put in more hours on the job
- B. ask for additional office help
- C. begin to delegate more of his work
- D. inquire of his supervisor if the paperwork is really necessary

17. Assume that you are a supervisor. One of the workers under your supervision expresses his need to speak to you about a client who has been particularly uncooperative in providing information.
The MOST appropriate action for you to take FIRST would be to
    - A. agree to see the client for the worker in order to get the information
    - B. advise the worker to try several more times to get the information before he asks you for help
    - C. tell the worker you will go with him to see the client in order to observe his technique
    - D. ask the worker some questions in order to determine the type of help he needs in the situation

17._____

18. The supervisor who is MOST likely to achieve a high level of productivity from the professional employees under his supervision is the one who
    - A. watches their progress continuously
    - B. provides them with just enough information to carry out their assigned tasks
    - C. occasionally pitches in and helps them with their work
    - D. shares with them responsibility for setting work goals

18._____

19. Assume that there has been considerable friction for some time among the workers of a certain unit. The supervisor in charge of this unit becomes aware that the problem is getting serious as shown by increased absenteeism and lateness, loud arguments, etc.
Of the following, the BEST course of action for the supervisor to take FIRST is to
    - A. have a staff discussion about objectives and problems
    - B. seek out and penalize the apparent trouble-makers
    - C. set up and enforce stricter formal rules
    - D. discipline the next subordinate who causes friction

19._____

20. Assume that an employee under your supervision asks you for some blank paper and pencils to take home to her young grandson who, she says, delights in drawing.
The one of the following actions you SHOULD take is to
    - A. give her the material she wants and refrain from any comment
    - B. refuse her request and tell her that the use of office supplies for personal reasons is not proper
    - C. give her the material but suggest that she buy it next time
    - D. tell her to take the material herself since you do not want to know anything about the matter

20._____

21. A certain supervisor is given a performance evaluation by his superior. In it he is commended for his method of "delegation," a term that USUALLY refers to the action of
    A. determining the priorities for activities which must be completed
    B. assigning to subordinates some of the duties for which he is responsible
    C. standardizing operations in order to achieve results as close as possible to established goals
    D. dividing the activities necessary to achieve an objective into simple steps

21._____

22. A supervisor is approached by a subordinate who complains that a fellow worker is not assuming his share of the workload and is, therefore, causing more work for others in the office.
Of the following, the MOST appropriate action for the supervisor to take in response to this complaint is to tell the subordinate
    A. that he will look into the matter
    B. to concentrate on his own job and not to worry about others
    C. to discuss the matter with the other worker
    D. that not everyone is capable of working at the same pace

22._____

23. Aside from the formal relationships established by management, informal and unofficial relationships will be developed among the personnel within an organization.
Of the following, the MAIN importance of such informal relationships to the operations of the formal organization is that they
    A. reinforce the basic goals of the formal organization
    B. insure the interchangeability of the personnel within the organization
    C. provide an additional channel of communications within the organization
    D. insure predictability and control of the behavior of members of the organization

23._____

24. The most productive worker in a unit frequently takes overly-long coffee breaks and lunch hours while maintaining his above-average rate of productivity.
Of the following, it would be MOST advisable for the supervisor to
    A. reprimand him, because rules must be enforced equally regardless of the merit of an individual's job performance
    B. ignore the infractions because a superior worker should be granted extra privileges for his efforts
    C. take no action unless others in the unit complain, because a reprimand may hurt the superior worker's feelings and cause him to produce less
    D. tell other members of the unit that a comparable rate of productivity on their part will be rewarded with similar privileges

24._____

25. A supervisor has been asked by his superior to choose an employee to supervise a special project.
Of the following, the MOST significant factor to consider in making this choice is the employee's
   A. length of service
   B. ability to do the job
   C. commitment to the goals of the agency
   D. attitude toward his fellow workers

KEY (CORRECT ANSWERS)

1.	B	11.	B
2.	A	12.	A
3.	C	13.	B
4.	D	14.	B
5.	A	15.	C
6.	C	16.	C
7.	D	17.	D
8.	A	18.	D
9.	B	19.	A
10.	B	20.	B

21.	B
22.	A
23.	C
24.	A
25.	B

TEST 4

DIRECTIONS: Each question or incomplete statement is followed by several suggested answers or completions. Select the one that BEST answers the question or completes the statement. *PRINT THE LETTER OF THE CORRECT ANSWER IN THE SPACE AT THE RIGHT.*

1. Assume that you are a newly appointed supervisor.
   Your MOST important responsibility is to
   A. make certain that all of the employees under your supervision are treated equally
   B. reduce disciplinary situations to a minimum
   C. insure an atmosphere of mutual trust between your workers and yourself
   D. see that the required work is done properly

   1._____

2. In order to make sure that work is completed on time, the supervisor should
   A. pitch in and do as much of the work herself as she can
   B. schedule the work and control its progress
   C. not assign more than one person to any one task
   D. assign the same amount of work to each subordinate

   2._____

3. Assume that you are a supervisor in charge of a number of workers who do the same kind of work and who each produce about the same volume of work in a given period of time.
   When their performance is evaluated, the worker who should be rated as the MOST accurate is the one
   A. whose errors are the easiest to correct
   B. whose errors involve the smallest amount of money
   C. who makes the fewest errors in her work
   D. who makes fewer errors as she becomes more experienced

   3._____

4. As a supervisor, you have been asked by the manager to recommend whether the work of the bookkeeping office requires a permanent increase in bookkeeping office staff.
   Of the following questions, the one whose answer would be MOST likely to assist you in making your recommendation is:
   A. Are temporary employees hired to handle seasonal fluctuations in work loads?
   B. Are some permanent employees working irregular hours because they occasionally work overtime?
   C. Are the present permanent employees keeping the work of the bookkeeping office current?
   D. Are employees complaining that the work is unevenly divided?

   4._____

5. Assume that you are a supervisor. One of your subordinates tells you that he is dissatisfied with his work assignment and that he wishes to discuss the matter with you. The employee is obviously very angry and upset.
Of the following, the course of action that you should take FIRST in this situation is to
   A. promise the employee that you will review all the work assignments in the office to determine whether any changes should be made.
   B. have the employee present his complaint, correcting him whenever he makes what seems to be an erroneous charge against you
   C. postpone discussion of the employee's complaint, explaining to him that the matter can be settled more satisfactory if it is discussed calmly
   D. permit the employee to present his complaint in full, withholding your comments until he has finished making his complaint

6. Assume that you are a supervisor. You find that you are spending too much time on routine tasks and not enough time on supervision of the work of your subordinates.
It would be ADVISABLE for you to
   A. assign some of the routine tasks to your subordinates
   B. postpone the performance of routine tasks until you have completed your supervisory tasks
   C. delegate the supervisory work to a capable subordinate
   D. eliminate some of the supervisory tasks that you are required to perform

7. Assume that you are a supervisor. You discover that one of your workers has violated an important rule.
The FIRST course of action for you as the supervisor to take would be to
   A. call a meeting of the entire staff and discuss the matter generally without mentioning any employee by name
   B. arrange to supervise the offending worker's activities more closely
   C. discuss the violation privately with the worker involved
   D. discuss the matter with the worker within hearing of the entire staff so that she will feel too ashamed to commit this violation in the future

8. As a supervisor, you are to prepare a vacation schedule for the bookkeeping office employees.
The one of the following that is the LEAST important factor for you to consider in setting up this schedule is
   A. seniority   B. vacation preferences of employees
   C. average productivity of the office

9. In assigning a complicated task to a group of subordinates, a certain supervisor does not indicate the specific steps to be followed in performing the assignment, nor does he designate which subordinate is to be responsible for seeing that the task is done on time.

This supervisor's method of assigning the task is MOST likely to result in
- A. confusion among subordinates with consequent delays in work
- B. greater individual effort and self-reliance
- C. assumption of authority by capable subordinates
- D. loss of confidence by subordinates in their ability

10. While you are explaining a new procedure to an employee, she asks you a question about the procedure which you cannot answer.
The MOST appropriate action for you to take is to
    - A. admit your inability to answer the question and promise to obtain the information
    - B. point out the likelihood of a situation arising which would require an answer to the question
    - C. ask the worker to give her reason for asking the question before you give any further reply
    - D. tell her to inform you immediately should a situation arise requiring an answer to her question

KEY (CORRECT ANSWERS)

1.	D	6.	A
2.	B	7.	C
3.	C	8.	C
4.	C	9.	A
5.	D	10.	A

REPORT WRITING

EXAMINATION SECTION

TEST 1

DIRECTIONS: Each question or incomplete statement is followed by several suggested answers or completions. Select the one that BEST answers the question or completes the statement. *PRINT THE LETTER OF THE CORRECT ANSWER IN THE SPACE AT THE RIGHT.*

1. Following are six steps that should be taken in the course of report preparation:
   I. Outlining the material for presentation in the report
   II. Analyzing and interpreting the facts
   III. Analyzing the problem
   IV. Reaching conclusions
   V. Writing, revising, and rewriting the final copy
   VI. Collecting data

   According to the principles of good report writing, the CORRECT order in which these steps should be taken is:
   A. VI, III, II, I, IV, V
   B. III, VI, II, IV, I, V
   C. III, VI, II, I, IV, V
   D. VI, II, III, IV, I, V

   1.____

2. Following are three statements concerning written reports:
   I. Clarity is generally more essential in oral reports than in written reports.
   II. Short sentences composed of simple words are generally preferred to complex sentences and difficult words.
   III. Abbreviations may be used whenever they are customary and will not distract the attention of the reader.

   Which of the following choices correctly classifies the above statements in to those which are valid and those which are not valid?
   A. I and II are valid, but III is not valid
   B. I is valid, but II and III are not valid.
   C. II and III are valid, but I is not valid.
   D. III is valid, but I and II are not valid.

   2.____

3. In order to produce a report written in a style that is both understandable and effective, an investigator should apply the principles of unit, coherence, and emphasis.
   The one of the following which is the BEST example of the principle of coherence is
   A. interlinking sentences so that thoughts flow smoothly
   B. having each sentence express a single idea to facilitate comprehension
   C. arranging important points in prominent positions so they are not overlooked
   D. developing the main idea fully to insure complete consideration

   3.____

4. Assume that a supervisor is preparing a report recommending that a standard work procedure be changed.
   Of the following, the MOST important information that he should include in this report is
   A. a complete description of the present procedure
   B. the details and advantages of the recommended procedure
   C. the type and amount of retraining needed
   D. the percentage of men who favor the change

5. When you include in your report on an inspection some information which you have obtained from other individuals, it is MOST important that
   A. this information have no bearing on the work these other people are performing
   B. you do not report as fact the opinions of other individuals
   C. you keep the source of the information confidential
   D. you do not tell the other individuals that their statements will be included in your report

6. Before turning in a report of an investigator of an accident, you discover some additional information you did not know about when you wrote the report. Whether or not you re-write your report to include this additional information should depend MAINLY on the
   A. source of this additional information
   B. established policy covering the subject matter of the report
   C. length of the report and the time it would take you to re-write it
   D. bearing this additional information will have on the conclusions in the report

7. The MOST desirable *first* step in the planning of a written report is to
   A. ascertain what necessary information is readily available in the files
   B. outline the methods you will employ to get the necessary information
   C. determine the objectives and uses of the report
   D. estimate the time and cost required to complete the report

8. In writing a report, the practice of taking up the least important points and the most important points last is a
   A. *good* technique since the final points made in a report will make the greatest impression on the reader
   B. *good* technique since the material is presented in a more logical manner and will lead directly to the conclusions
   C. *poor* technique since the reader's time is wasted by having to review irrelevant information before finishing the report
   D. *poor* technique since it may cause the reader to lose interest in the report and arrive at incorrect conclusions about the report

9. Which one of the following serves as the BEST guideline for you to follow for effective written reports?
Keep sentences
   A. short and limit sentences to one thought
   B. short and use as many thoughts as possible
   C. long and limit sentences to one thought
   D. long and use as many thoughts as possible

10. One method by which a supervisor might prepare written reports to management is to begin with the conclusions, results, or summary, and to follow this with the supporting data.
The BEST reason why management may *prefer* this form of report is that
   A. management lacks the specific training to understand the data
   B. the data completely supports the conclusions
   C. time is saved by getting to the conclusions of the report first
   D. the data contains all the information that is required for making the conclusions

11. When making written reports, it is MOST important that they be
   A. well-worded   B. accurate as to the facts
   C. brief   D. submitted immediately

12. Of the following, the MOST important reason for a supervisor to prepare good written reports is that
   A. a supervisor is rated on the quality of his reports
   B. decisions are often made on the basis of the reports
   C. such reports take less time for superiors to review
   D. such reports demonstrate efficiency of department operations

13. Of the following, the BEST test of a good report is whether it
   A. provides the information needed
   B. shows the good sense of the writer
   C. is prepared according to a proper format
   D. is grammatical and neat

14. When a supervisor writes a report, he can BEST show that he has a understanding of the subject of the report by
   A. including necessary facts and omitting nonessential details
   B. using statistical data
   C. giving his conclusions but not the data on which they are based
   D. using a technical vocabulary

15. Suppose you and another supervisor on the same level are assigned to work together on a report. You disagree strongly with one of the recommendations the other supervisor wants to include in the report but you cannot change his views.

Of the following, it would be BEST that
- A. you refuse to accept responsibility for the report
- B. you ask that someone else be assigned to this project to replace you
- C. each of you state his own ideas about this recommendation in the report
- D. you give in to the other supervisor's opinion for the sake of harmony

16. Standardized forms are often provided for submitting reports. 16.____
Of the following, the MOST important advantage of using standardized forms for reports is that
- A. they take less time to prepare than individually written reports
- B. the person making the report can omit information he considers unimportant
- C. the responsibility for preparing these reports can be turned over to subordinates
- D. necessary information is less likely to be omitted

17. A report which may BEST be classed as a *periodic* report is one which 17.____
- A. requires the same type of information at regular intervals
- B. contains detailed information which is to be retained in permanent records
- C. is prepared whenever a special situation occurs
- D. lists information in graphic form

18. In the writing of reports or letters, the ideas presented in a paragraph are usually 18.____
of unequal importance and require varying degrees of emphasis.
All of the following are methods of placing extra stress on an idea EXCEPT
- A. repeating it in a number of forms
- B. placing it in the middle of the paragraph
- C. placing it either at the beginning or at the end of a paragraph
- D. underlining it

Questions 19-25.

DIRECTIONS: Questions 19 through 25 concern the subject of report writing and are based on the information and incidents described in the following paragraph. (In answering these questions, assume that the facts and incidents in the paragraph are true.)

On December 15, at 8 A.M., seven Laborers reported to Foreman Joseph Meehan in the Greenbranch Yard in Queens. Meehan instructed the men to load some 50-pound boxes of books on a truck for delivery to an agency building in Brooklyn. Meehan told the men that, because the boxes were rather heavy, two men should work together, helping each other lift and load each box. Since Michael Harper, one of the Laborers, was without a partner, Meehan helped him with the boxes for a while. When Meehan was called to the telephone in a nearby building, however, Harper decided to lift a box himself. He appeared able to lift the box, but, as he got the box halfway up, he cried out that he had a sharp pain in his back. Another Laborer, Jorge Ortiz, who was passing by, ran over to help Harper put the box down. Harper suddenly dropped the box, which fell on Ortiz' right foot. By this time, Meehan had come out of the building. He immediately helped get the box off Ortiz' foot and had both men lie down. Meehan covered the men with blankets and called an ambulance, which arrived a half hour later. At the hospital, the doctor said that the X-ray results showed that Ortiz' right foot was broken in three places.

19. What would be the BEST term to use in a report describing the injury of Jorge Ortiz?
    A. Strain   B. Fracture   C. Hernia   D. Hemorrhage

    19.____

20. Which of the following would be the MOST accurate summary for the Foreman to put in his report of the incident?
    A. Ortiz attempted to help Harper carry a box which was too heavy for one person, but Harper dropped it before Ortiz got there.
    B. Ortiz tried to help Harper carry a box but Harper got a pain in his back and accidentally dropped the box on Ortiz' foot.
    C. Harper refused to follow Meehan's orders and lifted a box too heavy for him; he deliberately dropped it when Ortiz tried to help him carry it.
    D. Harper lifted a box and felt a pain in his back; Ortiz tried to help Harper put the box down but Harper accidentally dropped it on Ortiz' foot.

    20.____

21. One of the Laborers at the scene of the accident was asked his version of the incident.
    Which information obtained from this witness would be LEAST important for including in the accident report?
    A. His opinion as to the cause of the accident
    B. How much of the accident he saw
    C. His personal opinion of the victims
    D. His name and address

    21.____

22. What should be the MAIN objective of writing a report about the incident described in the above paragraph? To
    A. describe the important elements in the accident situation
    B. recommend that such Laborers as Ortiz be advised not to interfere in another's work unless given specific instructions
    C. analyze the problems occurring when there are not enough workers to perform a certain task
    D. illustrate the hazards involved in performing routine everyday tasks

    22.____

23. Which of the following is information *missing* from the above passage but which *should* be included in a report of the incident? The
    A. name of the Laborer's immediate supervisor
    B. contents of the boxes
    C. time at which the accident occurred
    D. object or action that caused the injury to Ortiz' foot

    23.____

24. According to the description of the incident, the accident occurred because
    A. Ortiz attempted to help Harper who resisted his help
    B. Harper failed to follow instructions given him by Meehan
    C. Meehan was not supervising his men as closely as he should have
    D. Harper was not strong enough to carry the box once he lifted it

    24.____

25. Which of the following is MOST important for a foreman to avoid when writing up an official accident report?
    A. Using technical language to describe equipment involved in the accident
    B. Putting in details which might later be judged unnecessary
    C. Giving an opinion as to conditions that contributed to the accident
    D. Recommending discipline for employees who, in his opinion, caused the accident

KEY (CORRECT ANSWERS)

1.	B		11.	B
2.	C		12.	B
3.	A		13.	A
4.	B		14.	A
5.	B		15.	C
6.	D		16.	D
7.	C		17.	A
8.	D		18.	B
9.	A		19.	B
10.	C		20.	D

21.	C
22.	A
23.	C
24.	B
25.	D

TEST 2

DIRECTIONS: Each question or incomplete statement is followed by several suggested answers or completions. Select the one that BEST answers the question or completes the statement. *PRINT THE LETTER OF THE CORRECT ANSWER IN THE SPACE AT THE RIGHT.*

1. Lieutenant X is preparing a report to submit to his commanding officer in order to get approval of a plan of operation he has developed.
   The report starts off with the statement of the problem and continues with the details of the problem. It contains factual information gathered with the help of field and operational personnel. It contains a final conclusion and recommendation for action. The recommendation is supplemented by comments from other precinct staff members on how the recommendations will affect their areas of responsibility. The report also includes directives and general orders ready for the commanding officer's signature. In addition, it has two statements of objections presented by two precinct staff members.
   Which one of the following, if any, is either an item that Lieutenant X should have included in his report and which is not mentioned above, or is an item which Lieutenant X improperly did include in his report?
   A. Considerations of alternative courses of action and their consequences should have been covered in the report.
   B. The additions containing undocumented objections to the recommended course of action should not have been included as part of the report.
   C. A statement on the qualifications of Lieutenant X, which would support his expertness in the field under consideration, should have been included in the report.
   D. The directives and general orders should not have been prepared and included in the report until the commanding officer had approved the recommendations.
   E. None of the above, since Lieutenant X's report was both proper and complete.

   1._____

2. During a visit to a section, the district supervisor criticizes the method being used by the assistant foreman to prepare a certain report and orders him to modify the method. This change ordered by the district supervisor is in direct conflict with the specific orders of the foreman.
   In this situation, it would be BEST for the assistant foreman to
   A. change the method and tell the foreman about the change at the first opportunity
   B. change the method and rely on the district supervisor to notify the foreman
   C. report the matter to the foreman and delay the preparation of the report
   D. ask the district supervisor to discuss the matter with the foreman but use the old method for the time being

   2._____

3. A department officer should realize that the MOST usual reason for writing a report is to
   A. give orders and follow up their execution
   B. establish a permanent record
   C. raise questions
   D. supply information

4. A very important report which is being prepared by a department officer will soon be due on the desk of the district supervisor. No typing help is available at this time for the officer.
   For the officer to write out this report in longhand in such a situation would be
   A. *bad*; such a report would not make the impression a typed report would
   B. *good*; it is important to get the report in on time
   C. *bad*; the district supervisor should not be required to read longhand reports
   D. *good*; it would call attention to the difficult conditions under which this section must work

5. In a well-written report, the length of each paragraph in the report should be
   A. varied according to the content
   B. not over 300 words
   C. pretty nearly the same
   D. gradually longer as the report is developed and written

6. A clerk in the headquarters office complains to you about the way in which you are filing out a certain report.
   It would be BEST for you to
   A. tell the clerk that you are following official procedures in filling out the report
   B. ask to be referred to the clerk's superior
   C. ask the clerk exactly what is wrong with the way in which you are filling out the report
   D. tell the clerk that you are following the directions of the district supervisor

7. The use of an outline to help in writing a report is
   A. *desirable*, in order to insure good organization and coverage
   B. *necessary*, so it can be used as an introduction to the report itself
   C. *undesirable*, since it acts as a straightjacket and may result in an unbalanced report
   D. *desirable*, if you know your immediate supervisor reads reports with extreme care and attention

8. It is advisable that a department officer do his paper work and report writing as soon as he has completed an inspection MAINLY because
   A. there are usually deadlines to be met
   B. it insures a steady work-flow
   C. he may not have time for this later
   D. the facts are then freshest in his mind

9. Before you turn in a report you have written of an investigation that you have made, you discover some additional information you didn't know about before. Whether or not you re-write the report to include this additional information should depend MAINLY on the
   A. amount of time remaining before the report is due
   B. established policy of the department covering the subject matter of the report
   C. bearing this information will have on the conclusions of the report
   D. number of people who will eventually review the report

9.____

10. When a supervisory officer submits a periodic report to the district supervisor, he should realize that the CHIEF importance of such a report is that it
    A. is the principal method of checking on the efficiency of the supervisor and his subordinates
    B. is something to which frequent reference will be made
    C. eliminates the need for any personal follow-up or inspection by higher echelons
    D. permits the district supervisor to exercise his functions of direction, supervision, and control better

10.____

11. Conclusions and recommendations are usually placed at the end rather than at the beginning of a report because
    A. the person preparing the report may decide to change some of the conclusions and recommendations before he reaches the end of the report
    B. they are the most important part of the report
    C. they can be judged better by the person to whom the report is sent after he reads the facts and investigators which come earlier in the report
    D. they can be referred to quickly when needed without reading the rest of the report

11.____

12. The use of the same method of record-keeping and reporting by all agency sections is
    A. *desirable*, MAINLY because it saves time in section operations
    B. *undesirable*, MAINLY because it kills the initiative of the individual section foreman
    C. *desirable*, MAINLY because it will be easier for the administrator to evaluate and compare section operations
    D. *undesirable*, MAINLY because operations vary from section to section and uniform record-keeping and reporting is not appropriate

12.____

13. The GREATEST benefit the section officer will have from keeping complete and accurate records and reports of section operations is that
    A. he will find it easier to run his section efficiently
    B. he will need less equipment
    C. he will need less manpower
    D. the section will run smoothly when he is out

13.____

14. You have prepared a report to your superior and are ready to send it forward. But on re-reading it, you think some parts are not clearly expressed and your superior ay have difficulty getting your point.
Of the following, it would be BEST for you to
    A. give the report to one of your men to read, and if he has no trouble understanding it send it through
    B. forward the report and call your superior the next day to ask whether it was all right
    C. forward the report as is; higher echelons should be able to understand any report prepared by a section officer
    D. do the report over, re-writing the sections you are in doubt about

14._____

15. The BEST of the following statements concerning reports is that
    A. a carelessly written report may give the reader an impression of inaccuracy
    B. correct grammar and English are unimportant if the main facts are given
    C. every man should be required to submit a daily work report
    D. the longer and more wordy a report is, the better it will read

15._____

16. In writing a report, the question of whether or not to include certain material could be determined BEST by considering the
    A. amount of space the material will occupy in the report
    B. amount of time to be spent in gathering the material
    C. date of the material
    D. value of the material to the superior who will read the report

16._____

17. Suppose you are submitting a fairly long report to your superior.
The one of the following sections that should come FIRST in this report is a
    A. description of how you gathered material
    B. discussion of possible objections to your recommendations
    C. plan of how your recommendations can be put into practice
    D. statement of the problem dealt with

17._____

Questions 18-20.

DIRECTIONS: A foreman is asked to write a report on the incident described in the following passage. Answer Questions 18 through 20 based on the following information.

On March 10, Henry Moore, a laborer, was in the process of transferring some equipment from the machine shop to the third floor. He was using a dolly to perform this task and, as he was wheeling the material through the machine shop, laborer Bob Greene called to him. As Henry turned to respond to Bob, he jammed the dolly into Larry Mantell's leg, knocking Larry down in the process and causing the heavy drill that Larry was holding to fall on Larry's foot. Larry started rubbing his foot and then, infuriated, jumped up and punched Henry in the jaw. The force of the blow drove Henry's head back against the wall. Henry did not fight back; he appeared to be dazed. An ambulance was called to take Henry to the hospital, and the ambulance attendant told the foreman that it appeared likely that Henry had suffered a concussion. Larry's injuries consisted of some bruises, but he refused medical attention.

18. An adequate report of the above incident should give as minimum information the names of the persons involved, the names of the witnesses, the date and the time that each event took place, and the
    A. names of the ambulance attendants
    B. names of all the employees working in the machine shop
    C. location where the accident occurred
    D. nature of the previous safety training each employee had been given

19. The only one of the following which is NOT a fact is
    A. Bob called to Henry
    B. Larry suffered a concussion
    C. Larry rubbed his foot
    D. the incident took place in the machine shop

20. Which of the following would be the MOST accurate summary of the incident for the foreman to put in his report of the accident?
    A. Larry Mantell punched Henry Moore because a drill fell on his foot and he was angry. Then Henry fell and suffered a concussion.
    B. Henry Moore accidentally jammed a dolly into Larry Mantell's foot, knocking Larry down. Larry punched Henry, pushing him into the wall and causing him to bang his head against the wall.
    C. Bob Greene called Henry Moore. A dolly than jammed into Larry Mantell and knocked him down. Larry punched Henry who tripped and suffered some bruises. An ambulance was called.
    D. A drill fell on Larry Mantell's foot. Larry jumped up suddenly and punched Henry Moore and pushed him into the wall. Henry may have suffered a concussion as a result of falling.

Questions 21-25.

DIRECTIONS: Questions 21 through 25 are to be answered ONLY on the basis of the information provided in the following passage.

A written report is a communication of information from one person to another. It is an account of some matter especially investigated, however routine that matter may be. The ultimate basis of any good written report is facts, which become known through observation and verification. Good written reports may seem to be no more than general ideas and opinions. However, in such cases, the facts leading to these opinions were gathered, verified, and reported earlier, and the opinions are dependent upon these facts. Good style, proper form, and emphasis cannot make a good written report out of unreliable information and bad judgment; but, on the other hand, solid investigation and brilliant thinking are not likely to become very useful until they are effectively communicated to others. If a person's work calls for written reports, then his work is often no better than his written reports.

6 (#2)

21. Based on the information in the above passage, it can be concluded that opinions expressed in a report should be
    A. based on facts which are gathered and reported
    B. emphasized repeatedly when they result from a special investigation
    C. kept to a minimum
    D. separated from the body of the report

    21._____

22. In the above passage, the one of the following which is mentioned as a way of establishing facts is
    A. authority
    B. communication
    C. reporting
    D. verification

    22._____

23. According to the above passage, the characteristic shared by ALL written reports is that they are
    A. accounts of routine matters
    B. transmissions of information
    C. reliable and logical
    D. written in proper form

    23._____

24. Which of the following conclusions can logically be drawn from the information given in the above passage?
    A. Brilliant thinking can make up for unreliable information in a report.
    B. One method of judging an individual's work is the quality of the written reports he is required to submit.
    C. Proper form and emphasis can make a good report out of unreliable information.
    D. Good written reports that seem to be no more than general ideas should be rewritten.

    24._____

25. Which of the following suggested titles would be MOST appropriate for this passage?
    A. Gathering and Organizing Facts
    B. Techniques of Observation
    C. Nature and Purpose of Reports
    D. Reports and Opinions: Differences and Similarities

    25._____

KEY (CORRECT ANSWERS)

1.	A	11.	C
2.	A	12.	C
3.	D	13.	A
4.	B	14.	D
5.	A	15.	A
6.	C	16.	D
7.	A	17.	D
8.	D	18.	C
9.	C	19.	B
10.	D	20.	B

21. A
22. D
23. B
24. B
25. C

TEST 3

DIRECTIONS: Each question or incomplete statement is followed by several suggested answers or completions. Select the one that BEST answers the question or completes the statement. *PRINT THE LETTER OF THE CORRECT ANSWER IN THE SPACE AT THE RIGHT.*

Questions 1-5.

DIRECTIONS: The following is an accident report similar to those used in departments for reporting accidents. Questions 1 through 5 are be answered using ONLY the information given in this report.

ACCIDENT REPORT

FROM: John Doe	DATE OF REPORT: June 23
TITLE: Sanitation Worker	
DATE OF ACCIDENT: June 22 time 3 ~~AM~~ PM	CITY: Metropolitan
PLACE: 1489 Third Avenue	
VEHICLE NO. 1	VEHICLE NO. 2
OPERATOR: John Doe, Sanitation Worker Title	OPERATOR: Richard Roe
VEHICLE CODE NO: 14-238	ADDRESS: 498 High Street
LICENSE NO.: 0123456	OWNER: Henry Roe ADDRESS: 786 E.83 St. LIC. NO.: 5N1492
DESCRIPTION OF ACCIDENT: Light green Chevrolet sedan while trying to pass drove in to rear side of sanitation truck which had stopped to collect garbage. No one was injured but there was property damage.	
NATURE OF DAMAGE TO PRIVATE VEHICLE: Right front fender crushed, bumper bent	
DAMAGE TO CITY VEHICLE: Front of left rear fender pushed in. Paint scraped.	
NAME OF WITNESS: Frank Brown	ADDRESS: 48 Kingsway
SIGNATURE OF PERSON MAKING THIS REPORT *John Doe*	BADGE NO.: 428

1. Of the following, the one which has been omitted from this accident report is the
    A. location of the accident
    B. drivers of the vehicles involved
    C. traffic situation at the time of the accident
    D. owners of the vehicles involved

    1.____

2. The address of the driver of Vehicle No. 1 is not required because he
    A. is employed by the department
    B. is not the owner of the vehicle
    C. reported the accident
    D. was injured in the accident

    2.____

3. The report indicates that the driver of Vehicle No. 2 was PROBABLY
    A. passing on the wrong side of the truck
    B. not wearing his glasses
    C. not injured in the accident
    D. driving while intoxicated

    3.____

150

4. The number of people *specifically* referred to in this report is 4.____
    A. 3   B. 4   C. 5   D. 6

5. The license number of Vehicle No. 1 is 5.____
    A. 428   B. 5N1492   C. 14-238   D. 0123456

6. In a report of unlawful entry into department premises, it is LEAST important to include the 6.____
    A. estimated value of the property missing
    B. general description of the premises
    C. means used to get into the premises
    D. time and date of entry

7. In a report of an accident, it is LEAST important to include the 7.____
    A. name of the insurance company of the person injured in the accident
    B. probable cause of the accident
    C. time and place of the accident
    D. names and addresses of all witnesses of the accident

8. Of the following, the one which is NOT required in the preparation of a weekly functional expense report is the 8.____
    A. hourly distribution of the time by proper heading in accordance with the actual work performed
    B. signatures of officers not involved in the preparation of the report
    C. time records of the men who appear on the payroll of the respective locations
    D. time records of men working in other districts assigned to this location

KEY (CORRECT ANSWERS)

1.	C	5.	D
2.	A	6.	B
3.	C	7.	A
4.	B	8.	B

PRINCIPLES AND PRACTICES, OF ADMINISTRATION, SUPERVISION AND MANAGEMENT

TABLE OF CONTENTS

	Page
GENERAL ADMINISTRATION	1
SEVEN BASIC FUNCTIONS OF THE SUPERVISOR	2
I. Planning	2
II. Organizing	3
III. Staffing	3
IV. Directing	3
V. Coordinating	3
VI. Reporting	3
VII. Budgeting	3
PLANNING TO MEET MANAGEMENT GOALS	4
I. What is Planning	4
II. Who Should Make Plans	4
III. What are the Results of Poor Planning	4
IV. Principles of Planning	4
MANAGEMENT PRINCIPLES	5
I. Management	5
II. Management Principles	5
III. Organization Structure	6
ORGANIZATION	8
I. Unity of Command	8
II. Span of Control	8
III. Uniformity of Assignment	9
IV. Assignment of Responsibility and Delegation of Authority	9
PRINCIPLES OF ORGANIZATION	9
I. Definition	9
II. Purpose of Organization	9
III. Basic Considerations in Organizational Planning	9
IV. Bases for Organization	10
V. Assignment of Functions	10
VI. Delegation of Authority and Responsibility	10
VII. Employee Relationships	11

DELEGATING		11
I.	WHAT IS DELEGATING:	11
II.	TO WHOM TO DELEGATE	11
REPORTS		12
I.	DEFINITION	12
II.	PURPOSE	12
III.	TYPES	12
IV.	FACTORS TO CONSIDER BEFORE WRITING REPORT	12
V.	PREPARATORY STEPS	12
VI.	OUTLINE FOR A RECOMMENDATION REPORT	12
MANAGEMENT CONTROLS		13
I.	Control	13
II.	Basis for Control	13
III.	Policy	13
IV.	Procedure	14
V.	Basis of Control	14
FRAMEWORK OF MANAGEMENT		14
I.	Elements	14
II.	Manager's Responsibility	15
III.	Control Techniques	16
IV.	Where Forecasts Fit	16
PROBLEM SOLVING		16
I.	Identify the Problem	16
II.	Gather Data	17
III.	List Possible Solutions	17
IV.	Test Possible Solutions	18
V.	Select the Best Solution	18
VI.	Put the Solution into Actual Practice	19
COMMUNICATION		19
I.	What is Communication?	19
II.	Why is Communication Needed?	19
III.	How is Communication Achieved?	20
IV.	Why Does Communication Fail?	21
V.	How to Improve Communication	21
VI.	How to Determine If You Are Getting Across	21
VII.	The Key Attitude	22
HOW ORDERS AND INSTRUCTIONS SHOULD BE GIVEN		22
I.	Characteristics of Good Orders and Instructions	22
FUNCTIONS OF A DEPARTMENT PERSONNEL OFFICE		23

SUPERVISION		23
I.	Leadership	23
	A. The Authoritarian Approach	23
	B. The Laissez-Faire Approach	24
	C. The Democratic Approach	24
II.	Nine Points of Contrast Between Boss and Leader	25
EMPLOYEE MORALE		25
I.	Some Ways to Develop and Maintain Good Employee Morale	25
II.	Some Indicators of Good Morale	26
MOTIVATION		26
EMPLOYEE PARTICIPATION		27
I.	WHAT IS PARTICIPATION	27
II.	WHY IS IT IMPORTANT?	27
III.	HOW MAY SUPERVISORS OBTAIN IT?	28
STEPS IN HANDLING A GRIEVANCE		28
DISCIPLINE		29
I.	THE DISCIPLINARY INTERVIEW	29
II.	PLANNING THE INTERVIEW	29
III.	CONDUCTING THE INTERVIEW	30

PRINCIPLES AND PRACTICES, OF ADMINISTRATION, SUPERVISION AND MANAGEMENT

Most people are inclined to think of administration as something that only a few persons are responsible for in a large organization. Perhaps this is true if you are thinking of Administration with a capital A, but administration with a lower case a is a responsibility of supervisors at all levels each working day.

All of us feel we are pretty good supervisors and that we do a good job of administering the workings of our agency. By and large, this is true, but every so often it is good to check up on ourselves. Checklists appear from time to time in various publications which psychologists say tell whether or not a person will make a good wife, husband, doctor, lawyer, or supervisor.

The following questions are an excellent checklist to test yourself as a supervisor and administrator.

Remember, Administration gives direction and points the way but administration carries the ideas to fruition. Each is dependent on the other for its success. Remember, too, that no unit is too small for these departmental functions to be carried out. These statements apply equally as well to the Chief Librarian as to the Department Head with but one or two persons to supervise.

GENERAL ADMINISTRATION: General Responsibilities of Supervisors

1. Have I prepared written statements of functions, activities, and duties for my organizational unit?

2. Have I prepared procedural guides for operating activities?

3. Have I established clearly in writing, lines of authority and responsibility for my organizational unit?

4. Do I make recommendations for improvements in organization, policies, administrative and operating routines and procedures, including simplification of work and elimination of non-essential operations?

5. Have I designated and trained an understudy to function in my absence?

6. Do I supervise and train personnel within the unit to effectively perform their assignments?

7. Do I assign personnel and distribute work on such a basis as to carry out the organizational unit's assignment or mission in the most effective and efficient manner?

8. Have I established administrative controls by:

    a. Fixing responsibility and accountability on all supervisors under my direction for the proper performance of their functions and duties.

b. Preparations and submitting periodic work load and progress reports covering the operations of the unit to my immediate superior.

c. Analysis and evaluation of such reports received from subordinate units.

d. Submission of significant developments and problems arising within the organizational unit to my immediate superior.

e. Conducting conferences, inspections, etc., as to the status and efficiency of unit operations.

9. Do I maintain an adequate and competent working force?

10. Have I fostered good employee-department relations, seeing that established rules, regulations, and instructions are being carried out properly?

11. Do I collaborate and consult with other organizational units performing related functions to insure harmonious and efficient working relationships?

12. Do I maintain liaison through prescribed channels with city departments and other governmental agencies concerned with the activities of the unit?

13. Do I maintain contact with and keep abreast of the latest developments and techniques of administration (professional societies, groups, periodicals, etc.) as to their applicability to the activities of the unit?

14. Do I communicate with superiors and subordinates through prescribed organizational channels?

15. Do I notify superiors and subordinates in instances where bypassing is necessary as soon thereafter as practicable?

16. Do I keep my superior informed of significant developments and problems?

SEVEN BASIC FUNCTIONS OF THE SUPERVISOR

I. PLANNING
This means working out goals and means to obtain goals. <u>What</u> needs to be done, <u>who</u> will do it, <u>how</u>, <u>when</u>, and <u>where</u> it is to be done.

SEVEN STEPS IN PLANNING

A. Define job or problem clearly.
B. Consider priority of job.
C. Consider time-limit—starting and completing.
D. Consider minimum distraction to, or interference with, other activities.
E. Consider and provide for contingencies—possible emergencies.
F. Break job down into components.

G. Consider the 5 W's and H:
   WHY..........is it necessary to do the job? (Is the purpose clearly defined?)
   WHAT........needs to be done to accomplish the defined purpose?
   ....is needed to do the job? (Money, materials, etc.)
   WHO..........is needed to do the job?
   ....will have responsibilities?
   WHERE......is the work to be done?
   WHEN........is the job to begin and end? (Schedules, etc.)
   HOW..........is the job to bed done? (Methods, controls, records, etc.)

II. ORGANIZING

This means dividing up the work, establishing clear lines of responsibility and authority and coordinating efforts to get the job done.

III. STAFFING

The whole personnel function of bringing in and <u>training</u> staff, getting the right man and fitting him to the right job—the job to which he is best suited.

In the normal situation, the supervisor's responsibility regarding staffing normally includes providing accurate job descriptions, that is, duties of the jobs, requirements, education and experience, skills, physical, etc.; assigning the work for maximum use of skills; and proper utilization of the probationary period to weed out unsatisfactory employees.

IV. DIRECTING

Providing the necessary leadership to the group supervised. Important work gets done to the supervisor's satisfaction.

V. COORDINATING

The all-important duty of inter-relating the various parts of the work.
The supervisor is also responsible for controlling the coordinated activities. This means measuring performance according to a time schedule and setting quotas to see that the goals previously set are being reached. Reports from workers should be analyzed, evaluated, and made part of all future plans.

VI. REPORTING

This means proper and effective communication to your superiors, subordinates, and your peers (in definition of the job of the supervisor). Reports should be read and information contained therein should be used, not be filed away and forgotten. Reports should be written in such a way that the desired action recommended by the report is forthcoming.

VII. BUDGETING
This means controlling current costs and forecasting future costs. This forecast is based on past experience, future plans and programs, as well as current costs.

You will note that these seven functions can fall under three topics:

Planning) Make a plan Staffing) Reporting) Watch it work
Organizing)   Directing) Get things done Budgeting)
                        Controlling)

PLANNING TO MEET MANAGEMENT GOALS

I. WHAT IS PLANNING?

   A. Thinking a job through before new work is done to determine the best way to do it
   B. A method of doing something
   C. Ways and means for achieving set goals
   D. A means of enabling a supervisor to deliver with a minimum of effort, all details involved in coordinating his work

II. WHO SHOULD MAKE PLANS?

   Everybody!
   All levels of supervision must plan work. (Top management, heads of divisions or bureaus, first line supervisors, and individual employees.) The higher the level, the more planning required.

III. WHAT ARE THE RESULTS OF POOR PLANNING?

   A. Failure to meet deadline
   B. Low employee morale
   C. Lack of job coordination
   D. Overtime is frequently necessary
   E. Excessive cost, waste of material and manhours

IV. PRINCIPLES OF PLANNING

   A. Getting a clear picture of your objectives. What exactly are you trying to accomplish?
   B. Plan the whole job, then the parts, in proper sequence.
   C. Delegate the planning of details to those responsible for executing them.
   D. Make your plan flexible.
   E. Coordinate your plan with the plans of others so that the work may be processed with a minimum of delay.
   F. Sell your plan before you execute it.
   G. Sell your plan to your superior, subordinate, in order to gain maximum participation and coordination.
   H. Your plan should take precedence. Use knowledge and skills that others have brought to a similar job.
   I. Your plan should take account of future contingencies; allow for future expansion.
   J. Plans should include minor details. Leave nothing to chance that can be anticipated.
   K. Your plan should be simple and provide standards and controls. Establish quality and quantity standards and set a standard method of doing the job. The controls will indicate whether the job is proceeding according to plan.
   L. Consider possible bottlenecks, breakdowns, or other difficulties that are likely to arise.

V. Q. WHAT ARE THE YARDSTICKS BY WHICH PLANNING SHOULD BE MEASURED?
    A. Any plan should:
       — Clearly state a definite course of action to be followed and goal to be achieved, with consideration for emergencies.
       — Be realistic and practical.
       — State what's to be done, when it's to be done, where, how, and by whom.
       — Establish the most efficient sequence of operating steps so that more is accomplished in less time, with the least effort, and with the best quality results.
       — Assure meeting deliveries without delays.
       — Establish the standard by which performance is to be judged.

    Q. WHAT KINDS OF PLANS DOES EFFECTIVE SUPERVISION REQUIRE?
    A. Plans should cover such factors as:
       — Manpower: right number of properly trained employees on the job
       — Materials: adequate supply of the right materials and supplies
       — Machines: full utilization of machines and equipment, with proper maintenance
       — Methods: most efficient handling of operations
       — Deliveries: making deliveries on time
       — Tools: sufficient well-conditioned tools
       — Layout: most effective use of space
       — Reports: maintaining proper records and reports
       — Supervision: planning work for employees and organizing supervisor's own time

MANAGEMENT PRINCIPLES

I. MANAGEMENT
    Q. What do we mean by management?
    A. Getting work done through others.

    Management could also be defined as planning, directing, and controlling the operations of a bureau or division so that all factors will function properly and all persons cooperate efficiently for a common objective.

II. MANAGEMENT PRINCIPLES

    A. There should be a hierarchy—wherein authority and responsibility run upward and downward through several levels—with a broad base at the bottom and a single head at the top.

    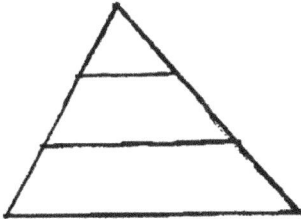

    B. Each and every unit or person in the organization should be answerable ultimately to the manager at the apex. In other words, *The buck stops here!*

C. Every necessary function involved in the bureau's objectives is assigned to a unit in that bureau.

D. Responsibilities assigned to a unit are specifically clear-cut and understood.

E. Consistent methods of organizational structure should be applied at each level of the organization.

F. Each member of the bureau from top to bottom knows: to whom he reports and who reports to him.

G. No member of one bureau reports to more than one supervisor. No dual functions.

H. Responsibility for a function is matched by authority necessary to perform that function. Weight of authority.

I. Individuals or units reporting to a supervisor do not exceed the number which can be feasibly and effectively coordinated and directed. Concept of *span of control*.

J. Channels of command (management) are not violated by staff units, although there should be staff services to facilitate and coordinate management functions.

K. Authority and responsibility should be decentralized to units and individuals who are responsible for the actual performance of operations.
Welfare – down to Welfare Centers
Hospitals – down to local hospitals

L. Management should exercise control through attention to policy problems of exceptional performance, rather than through review of routine actions of subordinates.

M. Organizations should never be permitted to grow so elaborate as to hinder work accomplishments.

III. ORGANIZATION STRUCTURE

Types of Organizations
The purest form is a leader and a few followers, such as:

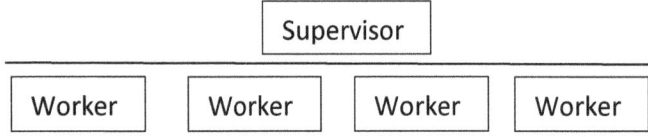

(Refer to organization chart) from supervisor to workers.

The line of authority is direct, The workers know exactly where they stand in relation to their boss, to whom they report for instructions and direction.

Unfortunately, in our present complex society, few organizations are similar to this example of a pure line organization. In this era of specialization, other people are often needed in the simplest of organizations. These specialists are known as staff. The sole purpose for their existence (staff) is to assist, advise, suggest, help or counsel line organizations. Staff has no authority to direct line people—nor do they give them direct instructions.

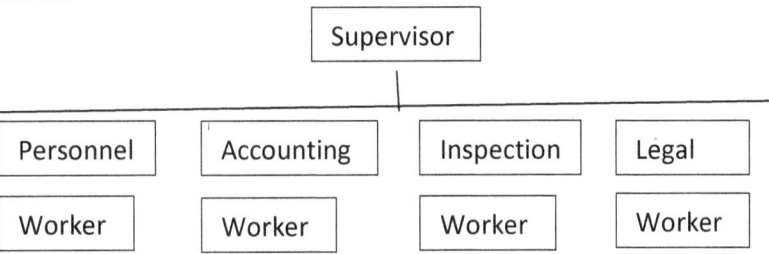

Line Functions
1. Directs
2. Orders
3. Responsibility for carrying out activities from beginning to end
4. Follows chain of command
5. Is identified with what it does
6. Decides when and how to use staff advice
7. Line executes

Staff Functions
1. Advises
2. Persuades and sells
3. Staff studies, reports, recommends but does not carry out
4. May advise across department lines
5. May find its ideas identified with others
6. Has to persuade line to want its advice
7. Staff: Conducts studies and research. Provides advice and instructions in technical matters. Serves as technical specialist to render specific services.

Types and Functions of Organization Charts
An organization chart is a picture of the arrangement and inter-relationship of the subdivisions of an organization.

A. Types of Charts:
   1. Structural: basic relationships only
   2. Functional: includes functions or duties
   3. Personnel: positions, salaries, status, etc.
   4. Process Chart: work performed
   5. Gantt Chart: actual performance against planned
   5. Flow Chart: flow and distribution of work

B. Functions of Charts:
   1. Assist in management planning and control
   2. Indicate duplication of functions
   3. Indicate incorrect stressing of functions
   4. Indicate neglect of important functions
   5. Correct unclear authority
   6. Establish proper span of control

C. Limitations of Charts:
1. Seldom maintained on current basis
2. Chart is oversimplified
3. Human factors cannot adequately be charted

D. Organization Charts should be:
1. Simple
2. Symmetrical
3. Indicate authority
4. Line and staff relationship differentiated
5. Chart should be dated and bear signature of approving officer
6. Chart should be displayed, not hidden

ORGANIZATION

There are four basic principles of organization:
1. Unity of command
2. Span of control
3. Uniformity of assignment
4. Assignment of responsibility and delegation of authority

I. UNITY OF COMMAND

Unity of command means that each person in the organization should receive orders from one, and only one, supervisor. When a person has to take orders from two or more people, (a) the orders may be in conflict and the employee is upset because he does not know which he should obey, or (b) different orders may reach him at the same time and he does not know which he should carry out first.

Equally as bad as having two bosses is the situation where the supervisor is bypassed. Let us suppose you are a supervisor whose boss bypasses you (deals directly with people reporting to you). To the worker, it is the same as having two bosses; but to you, the supervisor, it is equally serious. Bypassing on the part of your boss will undermine your authority, and the people under you will begin looking to your boss for decisions and even for routine orders.

You can prevent bypassing by telling the people you supervise that if anyone tries to give them orders, they should direct that person to you.

II. SPAN OF CONTROL

Span of control on a given level involves:
A. The number of people being supervised
B. The distance
C The time involved in supervising the people. (One supervisor cannot supervise too many workers effectively.)

Span of control means that a supervisor has the right number (not too many and not too few) of subordinates that he can supervise well.

III. UNIFORMITY OF ASSIGNMENT

In assigning work, you as the supervisor should assign to each person jobs that are similar in nature. An employee who is assigned too many different types of jobs will waste time in going from one kind of work to another. It takes time for him to get to top production in one kind of task and, before he does so, he has to start on another.
When you assign work to people, remember that:

A. Job duties should be definite. Make it clear from the beginning what they are to do, how they are to do it, and why they are to do it. Let them know how much they are expected to do and how well they are expected to do it.
B. Check your assignments to be certain that there are no workers with too many unrelated duties, and that no two people have been given overlapping responsibilities. Your aim should be to have every task assigned to a specific person with the work fairly distributed and with each person doing his part.

IV. ASSIGNMENT OF RESPONSIBILITY AND DELEGATION OF AUTHORITY

A supervisor cannot delegate his final responsibility for the work of his department. The experienced supervisor knows that he gets his work done through people. He can't do it all himself. So he must assign the work and the responsibility for the work to his employees. Then they must be given the authority to carry out their responsibilities.

By assigning responsibility and delegating authority to carry out the responsibility, the supervisor builds in his workers initiative, resourcefulness, enthusiasm, and interest in their work. He is treating them as responsible adults. They can find satisfaction in their work, and they will respect the supervisor and be loyal to the supervisor.

PRINCIPLES OF ORGANIZATION

I. DEFINITION

Organization is the method of dividing up the work to provide the best channels for coordinated effort to get the agency's mission accomplished.

II. PURPOSE OF ORGANIZATION

A. To enable each employee within the organization to clearly know his responsibilities and relationships to his fellow employees and to organizational units
B. To avoid conflicts of authority and overlapping of jurisdiction.
C. To ensure teamwork.

III. BASIC CONSIDERATIONS IIN ORGANIZATIONAL PLANNING

A. The basic plans and objectives of the agency should be determined, and the organizational structure should be adapted to carry out effectively such plans and objectives.
B. The organization should be built around the major functions of the agency and not individuals or groups of individuals.

C. The organization should be sufficiently flexible to meet new and changing conditions which may be brought about from within or outside the department.
D. The organizational structure should be as simple as possible and the number of organizational units kept at a minimum.
E. The number of levels of authority should be kept at a minimum. Each additional management level lengthens the chain of authority and responsibility and increases the time for instructions to be distributed to operating levels and for decisions to be obtained from higher authority.
F. The form of organization should permit each executive to exercise maximum initiative within the limits of delegated authority.

IV. BASES FOR ORGANIZATION

A. Purpose (Examples: education, police, sanitation)
B. Process (Examples: accounting, legal, purchasing)
C. Clientele (Examples: welfare, parks, veteran)
D. Geographic (Examples: borough offices, precincts, libraries)

V. ASSIGNMENTS OF FUNCTIONS

A. Every function of the agency should be assigned to a specific organizational unit. Under normal circumstances, no single function should be assigned to more than one organizational unit.
B. There should be no overlapping, duplication, or conflict between organizational elements.
C. Line functions should be separated from staff functions, and proper emphasis should be placed on staff activities.
D. Functions which are closely related or similar should normally be assigned to a single organizational unit.
E. Functions should be properly distributed to promote balance, and to avoid overemphasis of less important functions and underemphasis of more essential functions.

VI. DELEGATION OF AUTHORITY AND RESPONSIBILITY

A. Responsibilities assigned to a specific individual or organizational unit should carry corresponding authority, and all statements of authority or limitations thereof should be as specific as possible.
B. Authority and responsibility for action should be decentralized to organizational units and individuals responsible for actual performance to the greatest extent possible, without relaxing necessary control over policy or the standardization of procedures. Delegation of authority will be consistent with decentralization of responsibility but such delegation will not divest an executive in higher authority of his overall responsibility.
C. The heads of organizational units should concern themselves with important matters and should delegate to the maximum extent details and routines performed in the ordinary course of business.
D. All responsibilities, authorities, and relationships should be stated in simple language to avoid misinterpretation.
E. Each individual or organizational unit charged with a specific responsibility will be held responsible for results.

VII. EMPLOYEE RELATIONSHIPS

A. The employees reporting to one executive should not exceed the number which can be effectively directed and coordinated. The number will depend largely upon the scope and extent of the responsibilities of the subordinates.
B. No person should report to more than one supervisor. Every supervisor should know who reports to him, and every employee should know to whom he reports. Channels of authority and responsibility should not be violated by staff units.
C. Relationships between organizational units within the agency and with outside organizations and associations should be clearly stated and thoroughly understood to avoid misunderstanding.

DELEGATING

I. WHAT IS DELEGATING?
Delegating is assigning a job to an employee, giving him the authority to get that job done, and giving him the responsibility for seeing to it that the job is done.

A. What To Delegate
   1. Routine details
   2. Jobs which may be necessary and take a lot of time, but do not have to be done by the supervisor personally (preparing reports, attending meetings, etc.)
   3. Routine decision-making (making decisions which do not require the supervisor's personal attention)

B. What Not To Delegate
   1. Job details which are *executive functions* (setting goals, organizing employees into a good team, analyzing results so as to plan for the future)
   2. Disciplinary power (handling grievances, preparing service ratings, reprimands, etc.)
   3. Decision-making which involves large numbers of employees or other bureaus and departments
   4. Final and complete responsibility for the job done by the unit being supervised

C. Why Delegate?
   1. To strengthen the organization by developing a greater number of skilled employees
   2. To improve the employee's performance by giving him the chance to learn more about the job, handle some responsibility, and become more interested in getting the job done
   3. To improve a supervisor's performance by relieving him of routine jobs and giving him more time for *executive functions* (planning, organizing, controlling, etc.) which cannot be delegated

II. TO WHOM TO DELEGATE
People with abilities not being used. Selection should be based on ability, not on favoritism.

REPORTS

I. **DEFINITION**

A report is an orderly presentation of factual information directed to a specific reader for a specific purpose

II. **PURPOSE**

The general purpose of a report is to bring to the reader useful and factual information about a condition or a problem. Some specific purposes of a report may be:

A. To enable the reader to appraise the efficiency or effectiveness of a person or an operation
B. To provide a basis for establishing standards
C. To reflect the results of expenditures of time, effort, and money
D. To provide a basis for developing or altering programs

III. **TYPES**

A. Information Report: Contains facts arranged in sequence
B. Summary (Examination) Report: Contains facts plus an analysis or discussion of the significance of the facts. Analysis may give advantages and disadvantages or give qualitative and quantitative comparisons
C. Recommendation Report: Contains facts, analysis, and conclusion logically drawn from the facts and analysis, plus a recommendation based upon the facts, analysis, and conclusions

IV. **FACTORS TO CONSIDER BEFORE WRITING REPORT**

A. <u>Why</u> write the report?: The purpose of the report should be clearly defined.
B. <u>Who</u> will read the report?: What level of language should be used? Will the reader understand professional or technical language?
C. <u>What</u> should be said?: What does the reader need or want to know about the subject?
D. <u>How</u> should it be said?: Should the subject be presented tactfully? Convincingly? In a stimulating manner?

V. **PREPARATORY STEPS**

A. Assemble the facts: Find out who, why, what, where, when, and how.
B. Organize the facts: Eliminate unnecessary information
C. Prepare an outline: Check for orderliness, logical sequence
D. Prepare a draft: Check for correctness, clearness, completeness, conciseness, and tone
E. Prepare it in final form: Check for grammar, punctuation, appearance

VI. **OUTLINE FOR A RECOMMENDATION REPORT**

Is the report:
A. Correct in information, grammar, and tone?
B. Clear?
C. Complete?

D. Concise?
E. Timely?
F. Worth its cost?

Will the report accomplish its purpose?

MANAGEMENT CONTROLS

I. CONTROL
   What is control? What is controlled? Who controls?

   The essence of control is action which adjusts operations to predetermined standards, and its basis is information in the hands of managers. Control is checking to determine whether plans are being observed and suitable progress toward stated objectives is being made, and action is taken, if necessary, to correct deviations.

   We have a ready-made model for this concept of control in the automatic systems which are widely used for process control in the chemical land petroleum industries. A process control system works this way. Suppose, for example, it is desired to maintain a constant rate of flow of oil through a pipe at a predetermined or set-point value. A signal, whose strength represents the rate of flow, can be produced in a measuring device and transmitted to a control mechanism. The control mechanism, when it detects any deviation of the actual from the set-point signal, will reposition the value regulating flow rate.

II. BASIS FOR CONTROL

   A process control mechanism thus acts to adjust operations to predetermined standards and does so on the basis of information it receives. In a parallel way, information reaching a manager gives him the opportunity for corrective action and is his basis for control. He cannot exercise control without such information, and he cannot do a complete job of managing without controlling.

III. POLICY

   What is policy?

   Policy is simply a statement of an organization's intention to act in certain ways when specified types of circumstances arise. It represents a general decision, predetermined and expressed as a principle or rule, establishing a normal pattern of conduct for dealing with given types of business events—usually recurrent. A statement is therefore useful in economizing the time of managers and in assisting them to discharge their responsibilities equitably and consistently.

   Policy is not a means of control, but policy does generate the need for control.

   Adherence to policies is not guaranteed nor can it be taken on faith. It has to be verified. Without verification, there is no basis for control. Policy and procedures, although closely related and interdependent to a certain extent, are not synonymous. A policy may be adopted, for example, to maintain a materials inventory not to exceed one million dollars.

A procedure for inventory control could interpret that policy and convert it into methods for keeping within that limit, with consideration, too, of possible but foreseeable expedient deviation.

IV. PROCEDURE

What is procedure?

A procedure specifically prescribes:
A. What work is to be performed by the various participants
B. Who are the respective participants
C. When and where the various steps in the different processes are to be performed
D. The sequence of operations that will insure uniform handling of recurring transactions
E. The paper that is involved, its origin, transition, and disposition

Necessary appurtenances to a procedure are:
A. Detailed organizational chart
B. Flow charts
C. Exhibits of forms, all presented in close proximity to the text of the procedure

V. BASIS OF CONTROL – INFORMATION IN THE HANDS OF MANAGERS

If the basis of control is information in the hands of managers, then reporting is elevated to a level of very considerable importance.

Types of reporting may include:
A. Special reports and routine reports
B. Written, oral, and graphic reports
C. Staff meetings
D. Conferences
E. Television screens
F. Non-receipt of information, as where management is by exception
G. Any other means whereby information is transmitted to a manager as a basis for control action

FRAMEWORK OF MANAGEMENT

I. ELEMENTS

A. Policy: It has to be verified, controlled.

B. Organization is part of the giving of an assignment. The organizational chart gives to each individual in his title, a first approximation of the nature of his assignment and orients him as being accountable to a certain individual. Organization is not in a true sense a means of control. Control is checking to ascertain whether the assignment is executed as intended and acting on the basis of that information.

C. Budgets perform three functions:
1. They present the objectives, plans, and programs of the organization in financial terms.

2. They report the progress of actual performance against these predetermined objectives, plans, and programs.
3. Like organizational charts, delegations of authority, procedures, and job descriptions, they define the assignments which have flowed from the Chief Executive. Budgets are a means of control in the respect that they report progress of actual performance against the program. They provide information which enables managers to take action directed toward bringing actual results into conformity with the program.

D. Internal Check provides in practice for the principle that the same person should not have responsibility for all phases of a transaction. This makes it clearly an aspect of organization rather than of control. Internal Check is static, or built-in.

E. Plans, Programs, Objectives
People must know what they are trying to do. Objectives fulfill this need. Without them, people may work industriously and yet, working aimlessly, accomplish little. Plans and Programs complement Objectives, since they propose how and according to what time schedule the objectives are to be reached.

F. Delegations of Authority
Among the ways we have for supplementing the titles and lines of authority of an organizational chart are delegations of authority. Delegations of authority clarify the extent of authority of individuals and in that way serve to define assignments. That they are not means of control is apparent from the very fact that wherever there has been a delegation of authority, the need for control increases. This could hardly be expected to happen if delegations of authority were themselves means of control.

II. MANAGER'S RESPONSIBILITY

Control becomes necessary whenever a manager delegates authority to a subordinate because he cannot delegate and then simply sit back and forget4 about it. A manager's accountability to his own superior has not diminished one whit as a result of delegating part of his authority to a subordinate. The manager must exercise control over actions taken under the authority so delegated. That means checking serves as a basis for possible corrective action.

Objectives, plans, programs, organizational charts, and other elements of the managerial system are not fruitfully regarded as either controls or means of control. They are pre-established standards or models of performance to which operations are adjusted by the exercise of management control. These standards or models of performance are dynamic in character for they are constantly altered, modified, or revised. Policies, organizational set-up, procedures, delegations, etc. are constantly altered but, like objectives and plans, they remain in force until they are either abandoned or revised. All of the elements (or standards or models of performance), objectives, plans, and programs, policies, organization, etc. can be regarded as a *framework of management*.

III. CONTROL TECHNIQUES

Examples of control techniques:
A. Compare against established standards
B. Compare with a similar operation
C. Compare with past operations
D. Compare with predictions of accomplishment

IV. WHERE FORECASTS FIT

Control is after-the-fact while forecasts are before. Forecasts and projections are important for setting objectives and formulating plans.

Information for aiming and planning does not have to be before-the-fact. It may be an after-the-fact analysis proving that a certain policy has been impolitic in its effect on the relation of the company or department with customer, employee, taxpayer, or stockholder; or that a certain plan is no longer practical, or that a certain procedure is unworkable.

The prescription here certainly would not be in control (in these cases, control would simply bring operations into conformity with obsolete standards) but the establishment of new standards, a new policy, a new plan, and a new procedure to be controlled too.

Information is, of course, the basis for all communication in addition to furnishing evidence to management of the need for reconstructing the framework of management.

PROBLEM SOLVING

The accepted concept in modern management for problem solving is the utilization of the following steps:

A. Identify the problem
B. Gather data
C. List possible solutions
D. Test possible solutions
E. Select the best solution
F. Put the solution into actual practice

Occasions might arise where you would have to apply the second step of gathering data before completing the first step.

You might also find that it will be necessary to work on several steps at the same time.

I. IDENTIFY THE PROBLEM

Your first step is to define as precisely as possible the problem to be solved. While this may sound easy, it is often the most difficult part of the process.

It has been said of problem solving that you are halfway to the solution when you can write out a clear statement of the problem itself.

Our job now is to get below the surface manifestations of the trouble and pinpoint the problem. This is usually accomplished by a logical analysis, by going from the general to the particular; from the obvious to the not-so-obvious cause.

Let us say that production is behind schedule. WHY? Absenteeism is high. Now, is absenteeism the basic problem to be tackled, or is it merely a symptom of low morale among the workforce? Under these circumstances, you may decide that production is not the problem; the problem is *employee morale*.

In trying to define the problem, remember there is seldom one simple reason why production is lagging, or reports are late, etc.

Analysis usually leads to the discovery that an apparent problem is really made up of several subproblems which must be attacked separately.

Another way is to limit the problem, and thereby ease the task of finding a solution, and concentrate on the elements which are within the scope of your control.

When you have gone this far, write out a tentative statement of the problem to be solved.

II. GATHER DATA

In the second step, you must set out to collect all the information that might have a bearing on the problem. Do not settle for an assumption when reasonable fact and figures are available.

If you merely go through the motions of problem-solving, you will probably shortcut the information-gathering step. Therefore, do not stack the evidence by confining your research to your own preconceived ideas.

As you collect facts, organize them in some form that helps you make sense of them and spot possible relationships between them. For example, plotting cost per unit figures on a graph can be more meaningful than a long column of figures.

Evaluate each item as you go along. Is the source material absolutely, reliable, probably reliable, or not to be trusted.

One of the best methods for gathering data is to go out and look the situation over carefully. Talk to the people on the job who are most affected by this problem.

Always keep in mind that a primary source is usually better than a secondary source of information.

III. LIST POSSIBLE SOLUTIONS

This is the creative thinking step of problem solving. This is a good time to bring into play whatever techniques of group dynamics the agency or bureau might have developed for a joint attack on problems.

Now the important thing for you to do is: Keep an open mind. Let your imagination roam freely over the facts you have collected. Jot down every possible solution that occurs to you. Resist the temptation to evaluate various proposals as you go along. List seemingly absurd ideas along with more plausible ones. The more possibilities you list during this step, the less risk you will run of settling for merely a workable, rather than the best, solution.

Keep studying the data as long as there seems to be any chance of deriving additional ideas, solutions, explanations, or patterns from it.

IV. TEST POSSIBLE SOLUTIONS

Now you begin to evaluate the possible solutions. Take pains to be objective. Up to this point, you have suspended judgment but you might be tempted to select a solution you secretly favored all along and proclaim it as the best of the lot.

The secret of objectivity in this phase is to test the possible solutions separately, measuring each against a common yardstick. To make this yardstick try to enumerate as many specific criteria as you can think of. Criteria are best phrased as questions which you ask of each possible solution. They can be drawn from these general categories:

- Suitability – Will this solution do the job?
  Will it solve the problem completely or partially?
  Is it a permanent or a stopgap solution?

- Feasibility - Will this plan work in actual practice?
  Can we afford this approach?
  How much will it cost?

- Acceptability - Will the boss go along with the changes required in the plan?
  Are we trying to drive a tack with a sledge hammer?

V. SELECT THE BEST SOLUTION

This is the area of executive decision.

Occasionally, one clearly superior solution will stand out at the conclusion of the testing process. But often it is not that simple. You may find that no one solution has come through all the tests with flying colors.

You may also find that a proposal, which flunked miserably on one of the essential tests, racked up a very high score on others.

The best solution frequently will turn out to be a combination.

Try to arrange a marriage that will bring together the strong points of one possible solution with the particular virtues of another. The more skill and imagination that you apply, the greater is the likelihood that you will come out with a solution that is not merely adequate and workable, but is the best possible under the circumstances.

VI. PUT THE SOLUTION INTO ACTUAL PRACTICE

As every executive knows, a plan which works perfectly on paper may develop all sorts of bugs when put into actual practice.

Problem-solving does not stop with selecting the solution which looks best in theory. The next step is to put the chosen solution into action and watch the results. The results may point towards modifications.

If the problem disappears when you put your solution into effect, you know you have the right solution.

If it does not disappear, even after you have adjusted your plan to cover unforeseen difficulties that turned up in practice, work your way back through the problem-solving solutions.

> Would one of them have worked better?
> Did you overlook some vital piece of data which would have given you a different slant on the whole situation? Did you apply all necessary criteria in testing solutions? If no light dawns after this much rechecking, it is a pretty good bet that you defined the problem incorrectly in the first place.

You came up with the wrong solution because you tackled the wrong problem.

Thus, step six may become step one of a new problem-solving cycle.

COMMUNICATION

I. WHAT IS COMMUNICATION?

We communicate through writing, speaking, action, or inaction. In speaking to people face-to-face, there is opportunity to judge reactions and to adjust the message. This makes the supervisory chain one of the most, and in many instances the most, important channels of communication.

In an organization, communication means keeping employees informed about the organization's objectives, policies, problems, and progress. Communication is the free interchange of information, ideas, and desirable attitudes between and among employees and between employees and management.

II. WHY IS COMMUNICATION NEEDED?

A. People have certain social needs
B. Good communication is essential in meeting those social needs
C. While people have similar basic needs, at the same time they differ from each other
D. Communication must be adapted to these individual differences

An employee cannot do his best work unless he knows why he is doing it. If he has the feeling that he is being kept in the dark about what is going on, his enthusiasm and productivity suffer.

Effective communication is needed in an organization so that employees will understand what the organization is trying to accomplish; and how the work of one unit contributes to or affects the work of other units in the organization and other organizations.

III. HOW IS COMMUNICATION ACHIEVED?

Communication flows downward, upward, sideways.

   A. Communication may come from top management down to employees. This is downward communication.

   Some means of downward communication are:
   1. Training (orientation, job instruction, supervision, public relations, etc.)
   2. Conferences
   3. Staff meetings
   4. Policy statements
   5. Bulletins
   6. Newsletters
   7. Memoranda
   8. Circulation of important letters

   In downward communication, it is important that employees be informed in advance of changes that will affect them.

   B. Communications should also be developed so that the ideas, suggestions, and knowledge of employees will flow upward to top management.

   Some means of upward communication are:
   1. Personal discussion conferences
   2. Committees
   3. Memoranda
   4. Employees suggestion program
   5. Questionnaires to be filled in giving comments and suggestions about proposed actions that will affect field operations.

   Upward communication requires that management be willing to listen, to accept, and to make changes when good ideas are present. Upward communication succeeds when there is no fear of punishment for speaking out or lack of interest at the top. Employees will share their knowledge and ideas with management when interest is shown and recognition is given.

   C. The advantages of downward communication:
   1. It enables the passing down of orders, policies, and plans necessary to the continued operation of the station.
   2. By making information available, it diminishes the fears and suspicions which result from misinformation and misunderstanding.
   3. It fosters the pride people want to have in their work when they are told of good work.
   4. It improves the morale and stature of the individual to be *in the know*.

5. It helps employees to understand, accept, and cooperate with changes when they know about them in advance.

D. The advantages of upward communication:
1. It enables the passing upward of information, attitudes, and feelings.
2. It makes it easier to find out how ready people are to receive downward communication.
3. It reveals the degree to which the downward communication is understood and accepted.
4. It helps to satisfy the basic social needs.
5. It stimulates employees to participate in the operation of their organization.
6. It encourage employees to contribute ideas for improving the efficiency and economy of operations.
7. It helps to solve problem situations before they reach the explosion point.

IV. WHY DOES COMMUNICATION FAIL?

A. The technical difficulties of conveying information clearly
B. The emotional content of communication which prevents complete transmission
C. The fact that there is a difference between what management needs to say, what it wants to day, and what it does say
D. The fact that there is a difference between what employees would like to say, what they think is profitable or safe to say, and what they do say

V. HOW TO IMPROVE COMMUNICATION

As a supervisor, you are a key figure in communication. To improve as a communicator, you should:
A. Know: Knowing your subordinates will help you to recognize and work with individual differences.
B. Like: If you like those who work for you and those for whom you work, this will foster the kind of friendly, warm, work atmosphere that will facilitate communication.
C. Trust: Showing a sincere desire to communicate will help to develop the mutual trust and confidence which are essential to the free flow of communication.
D. Tell: Tell your subordinates and superiors *what's doing*. Tell your subordinates *why* as well as *how*.
E. Listen: By listening, you help others to talk and you create good listeners. Don't forget that listening implies action.
F. Stimulate: Communication has to be stimulated and encouraged. Be receptive to ideas and suggestions and motivate your people so that each member of the team identifies himself with the job at hand.
G. Consult: The most effective way of consulting is to let your people participate, insofar as possible, in developing determinations which affect them or their work.

VI. HOW TO DETERMINE WHETHER YOU ARE GETTING ACROSS

A. Check to see that communication is received and understood
B. Judge this understanding by actions rather than words
C. Adapt or vary communication, when necessary
D. Remember that good communication cannot cure all problems

VII. THE KEY ATTITUDE

Try to see things from the other person's point of view. By doing this, you help to develop the permissive atmosphere and the shared confidence and understanding which are essential to effective two-way communication.

Communication is a two-way process:
A. The basic purpose of any communication is to get action.
B. The only way to get action is through acceptance.
C. In order to get acceptance, communication must be humanly satisfying as well as technically efficient.

HOW ORDERS AND INSTRUCTIONS SHOULD BE GIVEN

I. CHARACTERISTICS OF GOOD ORDERS AND INSTRUCTIONS

  A. Clear
     Orders should be definite as to
     —What is to be done
     —Who is to do it
     —When it is to be done
     —Where it is to be done
     —How it is to be done

  B. Concise
     Avoid wordiness. Orders should be brief and to the point.

  C. Timely
     Instructions and orders should be sent out at the proper time and not too long in advance of expected performance.

  D. Possibility of Performance
     Orders should be feasible:
     1. Investigate before giving orders
     2. Consult those who are to carry out instructions before formulating and issuing them

  E. Properly Directed
     Give the orders to the people concerned. Do not send orders to people who are not concerned. People who continually receive instructions that are not applicable to them get in the habit of neglecting instructions generally.

  F. Reviewed Before Issuance
     Orders should be reviewed before issuance:
     1. Test them by putting yourself in the position of the recipient
     2. If they involve new procedures, have the persons who are to do the work review them for suggestions.

  G. Reviewed After Issuance
     Persons who receive orders should be allowed to raise questions and to point out unforeseen consequences of orders.

H. Coordinated
Orders should be coordinated so that work runs smoothly.

I. Courteous
Make a request rather than a demand. There is no need to continually call attention to the fact that you are the boss.

J. Recognizable as an Order
Be sure that the order is recognizable as such.

K. Complete
Be sure recipient has knowledge and experience sufficient to carry out order. Give illustrations and examples.

A DEPARTMENTAL PERSONNEL OFFICE IS RESPONSIBLE FOR THE FOLLOWING FUNCTIONS

1. Policy
2. Personnel Programs
3. Recruitment and Placement
4. Position Classification
5. Salary and Wage Administration
6. Employee performance Standards and Evaluation
7. Employee Relations
8. Disciplinary Actions and Separations
9. Health and Safety
10. Staff Training and Development
11. Personnel Records, Procedures, and Reports
12. Employee Services
13. Personnel Research

SUPERVISION

I. LEADERSHIP

All leadership is based essentially on authority. This comes from two sources: It is received from higher management or it is earned by the supervisor through his methods of supervision. Although effective leadership has always depended upon the leader's using his authority in such a way as to appeal successfully to the motives of the people supervised, the conditions for making this appeal are continually changing. The key to today's problem of leadership is flexibility and resourcefulness on the part of the leader in meeting changes in conditions as they occur.

Three basic approaches to leadership are generally recognized:

A. The Authoritarian Approach
1. The methods and techniques used in this approach emphasize the *I* in leadership and depend primarily on the formal authority of the leader. This authority is sometimes exercised in a hardboiled manner and sometimes in a benevolent

manner, but in either case the dominating role of the leader is reflected in the thinking, planning, and decisions of the group.
2. Group results are to a large degree dependent on close supervision by the leader. Usually, the individuals in the group will not show a high degree of initiative or acceptance of responsibility and their capacity to grow and develop probably will not be fully utilized. The group may react with resentment or submission, depending upon the manner and skill of the leader in using his authority.
3. This approach develops as a natural outgrowth of the authority that goes with the leader's job and his feeling of sole responsibility for getting the job done. It is relatively easy to use and does not require must resourcefulness.
4. The use of this approach is effective in times of emergencies, in meeting close deadline as a final resort, in settling some issues, in disciplinary matters, and with dependent individuals and groups.

B. The Laissez-Faire or Let 'em Alone Approach
1. This approach generally is characterized by an avoidance of leadership responsibility by the leader. The activities of the group depend largely on the choice of its members rather than the leader.
2. Group results probably will be poor. Generally, there will be disagreements over petty things, bickering, and confusion. Except for a few aggressive people, individuals will not show much initiative and growth and development will be retarded. There may be a tendency for informal leaders to take over leadership of the group.
3. This approach frequently results from the leader's dislike of responsibility, from his lack of confidence, from failure of other methods to work, from disappointment or criticism. It is usually the easiest of the three to use and requires both understanding and resourcefulness on the part of the leader.
4. This approach is occasionally useful and effective, particularly in forcing dependent individuals or groups to rely on themselves, to give someone a chance to save face by clearing his own difficulties, or when action should be delayed temporarily for good cause.

C. The Democratic Approach
1. The methods and techniques used in this approach emphasize the *we* in leadership and build up the responsibility of the group to attain its objectives. Reliance is placed largely on the earned authority of the leader.
2. Group results are likely to be good because most of the job motives of the people will be satisfied. Cooperation and teamwork, initiative, acceptance of responsibility, and the individual's capacity for growth probably will show a high degree of development.
3. This approach grows out of a desire or necessity of the leader to find ways to appeal effectively to the motivation of his group. It is the best approach to build up inside the person a strong desire to cooperate and apply himself to the job. It is the most difficult to develop, and requires both understanding and resourcefulness on the part of the leader.
4. The value of this approach increases over a long period where sustained efficiency and development of people are important. It may not be fully effective in all situations, however, particularly when there is not sufficient time to use it properly or where quick decisions must be made.

All three approaches are used by most leaders and have a place in supervising people. The extent of their use varies with individual leaders, with some using one approach predominantly. The leader who uses these three approaches, and varies their use with time and circumstance, is probably the most effective. Leadership which is used predominantly with a democratic approach requires more resourcefulness on the part of the leader but offers the greatest possibilities in terms of teamwork and cooperation.

The one best way of developing democratic leadership is to provide a real sense of participation on the part of the group, since this satisfies most of the chief job motives. Although there are many ways of providing participation, consulting as frequently as possible with individuals and groups on things that affect them seems to offer the most in building cooperation and responsibility. Consultation takes different forms, but it is most constructive when people feel they are actually helping in finding the answers to the problems on the job.

There are some requirements of leaders in respect to human relations which should be considered in their selection and development. Generally, the leader should be interested in working with other people, emotionally stable, self-confident, and sensitive to the reactions of others. In addition, his viewpoint should be one of getting the job done through people who work cooperatively in response to his leadership. He should have a knowledge of individual and group behavior, but, most important of all, he should work to combine all of these requirements into a definite, practical skill in leadership.

II. NINE POINTS OF CONTRAST BETWEEN *BOSS* AND *LEADER*

   A. The boss drives his men; the leader coaches them.
   B. The boss depends on authority; the leader on good will.
   C. The boss inspires fear; the leader inspires enthusiasm.
   D. The boss says I; the leader says *We*.
   E. The boss says *Get here on time*; the leader gets there ahead of time.
   F. The boss fixes the blame for the breakdown; the leader fixes the breakdown.
   G. The boss knows how it is done; the leader shows how.
   H. The boss makes work a drudgery; the leader makes work a game.
   I. The boss says *Go*; the leader says *Let's go*.

EMPLOYEE MORALE

Employee morale is the way employees feel about each other, the organization or unit in which they work, and the work they perform.

I. SOME WAYS TO DEVELOP AND MAINTAIN GOOD EMPLYEE MORALE

   A. Give adequate credit and praise when due.
   B. Recognize importance of all jobs and equalize load with proper assignments, always giving consideration to personality differences and abilities.
   C. Welcome suggestions and do not have an *all-wise* attitude. Request employees' assistance in solving problems and use assistants when conducting group meetings on certain subjects.
   D. Properly assign responsibilities and give adequate authority for fulfillment of such assignments.

E. Keep employees informed about matters that affect them.
F. Criticize and reprimand employees privately.
G. Be accessible and willing to listen.
H. Be fair.
I. Be alert to detect training possibilities so that you will not miss an opportunity to help each employee do a better job, and if possible with less effort on his part.
J. Set a good example.
K. Apply the golden rule.

II. SOME INDICATIONS OF GOOD MORALE

A. Good quality of work
B. Good quantity
C. Good attitude of employees
D. Good discipline
E. Teamwork
F. Good attendance
G. Employee participation

MOTIVATION

DRIVES

A drive, stated simply, is a desire or force which causes a person to do or say certain things. These are some of the most usual drives and some of their identifying characteristics recognizable in people motivated by such drives:

A. Security (desire to provide for the future)
Always on time for work
Works for the same employer for many years
Never takes unnecessary chances
Seldom resists doing what he is told

B. Recognition (desire to be rewarded for accomplishment)
Likes to be asked for his opinion
Becomes very disturbed when he makes a mistake
Does things to attract attention
Likes to see his name in print

C. Position (desire to hold certain status in relation to others)
Boasts about important people he knows
Wants to be known as a key man
Likes titles
Demands respect
Belongs to clubs, for prestige

D. Accomplishment (desire to get things done)
   Complains when things are held up
   Likes to do things that have tangible results
   Never lies down on the job
   Is proud of turning out good work

E. Companionship (desire to associate with other people)
   Likes to work with others
   Tells stories and jokes
   Indulges in horseplay
   Finds excuses to talk to others on the job

F. Possession (desire to collect and hoard objects)
   Likes to collect things
   Puts his name on things belonging to him
   Insists on the same location

Supervisors may find that identifying the drives of employees is a helpful step toward motivating them to self-improvement and better job performance. For example: An employee's job performance is below average. His supervisor, having previously determined that the employee is motivated by a drive for security, suggests that taking training courses will help the employee to improve, advance, and earn more money. Since earning more money can be a step toward greater security, the employee's drive for security would motivate him to take the training suggested by the supervisor. In essence, this is the process of charting an employee's future course by using his motivating drives to positive advantage.

EMPLOYEE PARTICIPATION

I. WHAT IS PARTICIPATION

Employee participation is the employee's giving freely of his time, skill, and knowledge to an extent which cannot be obtained by demand.

II. WHY IS IT IMPORTANT?

The supervisor's responsibility is to get the job done through people. A good supervisor gets the job done through people who work willingly and well. The participation of employees is important because:

A. Employees develop a greater sense of responsibility when they share in working out operating plans and goals.
B. Participation provides greater opportunity and stimulation for employees to learn, and to develop their ability.
C. Participation sometimes provides better solutions to problems because such solutions may combine the experience and knowledge of interested employees who want the solutions to work.
D. An employee or group may offer a solution which the supervisor might hesitate to make for fear of demanding too much.

E. Since the group wants to make the solution work, they exert pressure in a constructive way on each other.
F. Participation usually results in reducing the need for close supervision.

II. HOW MAY SUPERVISORS OBTAIN IT?

Participation is encouraged when employees feel that they share some responsibility for the work and that their ideas are sincerely wanted and valued. Some ways of obtaining employee participation are:

A. Conduct orientation programs for new employees to inform them about the organization and their rights and responsibilities as employees.
B. Explain the aims and objectives of the agency. On a continuing basis, be sure that the employees know what these aims and objectives are.
C. Share job successes and responsibilities and give credit for success.
D. Consult with employees, both as individuals and in groups, about things that affect them.
E. Encourage suggestions for job improvements. Help employees to develop good suggestions. The suggestions can bring them recognition. The city's suggestion program offers additional encouragement through cash awards.

The supervisor who encourages employee participation is not surrendering his authority. He must still make decisions and initiate action, and he must continue to be ultimately responsible for the work of those he supervises. But, through employee participation, he is helping his group to develop greater ability and a sense of responsibility while getting the job done faster and better.

STEPS IN HANDLING A GRIEVANCE

1. Get the Facts
    a. Listen sympathetically
    b. Let him talk himself out
    c. Get his story straight
    d. Get his point of view
    e. Don't argue with him
    f. Give him plenty of time
    g. Conduct the interview privately
    h. Don't try to shift the blame or pass the buck

2. Consider the Facts
    a. Consider the employee's viewpoint
    b. How will the decision affect similar cases
    c. Consider each decision as a possible precedent
    d. Avoid snap judgments—don't jump to conclusions

3. Make or Get a Decision
    a. Frame an effective counter-proposal
    b. Make sure it is fair to all
    c. Have confidence in your judgment
    d. Be sure you can substantiate your decision

4. Notify the Employee of Your Decision
   Be sure he is told; try to convince him that the decision is fair and just.

5. Take Action When Needed and If Within Your Authority
   Otherwise, tell employee that the matter will be called to the attention of the proper person or that nothing can be done, and why it cannot.

6. Follow through to see that the desired result is achieved.

7. Record key facts concerning the complaint and the action taken.

8. Leave the way open to him to appeal your decision to a higher authority.

9. Report all grievances to your superior, whether they are appealed or not.

DISCIPLINE

Discipline is training that develops self-control, orderly conduct, and efficiency.

To discipline does not necessarily mean to punish.

To discipline does mean to train, to regulate, and to govern conduct.

I. THE DISCIPLINARY INTERVIEW

Most employees sincerely want to do what is expected of them. In other words, they are self-disciplined. Some employees, however, fail to observe established rules and standards, and disciplinary action by the supervisor is required.

The primary purpose of disciplinary action is to improve conduct without creating dissatisfaction, bitterness, or resentment in the process.

Constructive disciplinary action is more concerned with causes and explanations of breaches of conduct than with punishment. The disciplinary interview is held to get at the causes of apparent misbehavior and to motivate better performance in the future.

It is important that the interview be kept on an impersonal a basis as possible. If the supervisor lets the interview descend to the plane of an argument, it loses its effectiveness.

II. PLANNING THE INTERVIEW

Get all pertinent facts concerning the situation so that you can talk in specific terms to the employee.

Review the employee's record, appraisal ratings, etc.

Consider what you know about the temperament of the employee. Consider your attitude toward the employee. Remember that the primary requisite of disciplinary action is fairness.

Don't enter upon the interview when angry.

Schedule the interview for a place which is private and out of hearing of others.

III. CONDUCTING THE INTERVIEW

    A. Make an effort to establish accord.
    B. Question the employee about the apparent breach of discipline. Be sure that the question is not so worded as to be itself an accusation.
    C. Give the employee a chance to tell his side of the story. Give him ample opportunity to talk.
    D. Use understanding—listening except where it is necessary to ask a question or to point out some details of which the employee may not be aware. If the employee misrepresents facts, make a plain, accurate statement of the facts, but don't argue and don't engage in personal controversy.
    E. Listen and try to understand the reasons for the employee's (mis)conduct. First of all, don't assume that there has been a breach of discipline. Evaluate the employee's reasons for his conduct in the light of his opinions and feelings concerning the consistency and reasonableness of the standards which he was expected to follow. Has the supervisor done his part in explaining the reasons for the rule? Was the employee's behavior unintentional or deliberate? Does he think he had real reasons for his actions? What new facts is he telling? Do the facts justify his actions? What causes, other than those mentioned, could have stimulated the behavior?
    F. After listening to the employee's version of the situation, and if censure of his actions is warranted, the supervisor should proceed with whatever criticism is justified. Emphasis should be placed on future improvement rather than exclusively on the employee's failure to measure up to expected standards of job conduct.
    G. Fit the criticism to the individual. With one employee, a word of correction may be all that is required.
    H. Attempt to distinguish between unintentional error and deliberate misbehavior. An error due to ignorance requires training and not censure.
    I. Administer criticism in a controlled, even tone of voice, never in anger. Make it clear that you are acting as an agent of the department. In general, criticism should refer to the job or the employee's actions and not to the person. Criticism of the employee's work is not an attack on the individual.
    J. Be sure the interview does not destroy the employee's self-confidence. Mention his good qualities and assure him that you feel confident that he can improve his performance.
    K. Wherever possible, before the employee leaves the interview, satisfy him that the incident is closed, that nothing more will be said on the subject unless the offense is repeated.

GLOSSARY OF PROJECT MANAGEMENT

A

Agile software development is a set of fundamental principles about how software should be developed based on an agile way of working in contrast to previous heavy-handed software development methodologies.

Aggregate planning is an operational activity which does an aggregate plan for the production process, in advance of 2 to 18 months, to give an idea to management as to what quantity of materials and other resources are to be procured and when, so that the total cost of operations of the organization is kept to the minimum over that period.

Allocation is the assignment of available resources in an economic way.

B

Budget generally refers to a list of all planned expenses and revenues.

Budgeted cost of work performed (BCWP) measures the budgeted cost of work that has actually been performed, rather than the cost of work scheduled.

Budgeted cost of work scheduled (BCWS) the approved budget that has been allocated to complete a scheduled task (or Work Breakdown Structure (WBS) component) during a specific time period.

Business model is a profit-producing system that has an important degree of independence from the other systems within an enterprise.

Business analysis is the set of tasks, knowledge, and techniques required to identify business needs and determine solutions to business problems. Solutions often include a systems development component, but may also consist of process improvement or organizational change.

Business operations are those ongoing recurring activities involved in the running of a business for the purpose of producing value for the stakeholders. They are contrasted with project management, and consist of business processes.

Business process is a collection of related, structured activities or tasks that produce a specific service or product (serve a particular goal) for a particular customer or customers. There are three types of business processes: Management processes, Operational processes, and Supporting processes.

Business Process Modeling (BPM) is the activity of representing processes of an enterprise, so that the current ("as is") process may be analyzed and improved in future ("to be").

C

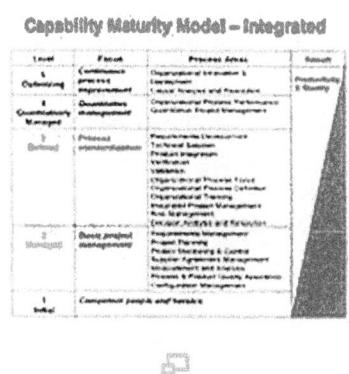

Capability Maturity Model.

Capability Maturity Model (CMM) in software engineering is a model of the maturity of the capability of certain business processes. A maturity model can be described as a structured collection of elements that describe certain aspects of maturity in an organization, and aids in the definition and understanding of an organization's processes.

Change control is the procedures used to ensure that changes (normally, but not necessarily, to IT systems) are introduced in a controlled and coordinated manner. Change control is a major aspect of the broader discipline of change management.

Change management is a field of management focused on organizational changes. It aims to ensure that methods and procedures are used for efficient and prompt handling of all changes to controlled IT infrastructure, in order to minimize the number and impact of any related incidents upon service.

Case study is a research method which involves an in-depth, longitudinal examination of a single instance or event: a case. They provide a systematic way of looking at events, collecting data, analyzing information, and reporting the results.

Certified Associate in Project Management is an entry-level certification for project practitioners offered by Project Management Institute.

Communications Log is an on-going documentation of communication events between any identified project stakeholders, managed and collected by the project manager that describes: the sender and receiver of the communication event; where, when and for how long the communication event elapsed; in what form the communication event took place; a summary of what information was communicated; what actions/outcomes should be taken as a result of the communication event; and to what level of priority should the actions/outcomes of the communication event be graded

Constructability is a project management technique to review the construction processes from start to finish during pre-construction phrase. It will identify obstacles before a project is actually built to reduce or prevent error, delays, and cost overrun.

Costs in economics, business, and accounting are the value of money that has been used up to produce something, and hence is not available for use anymore. In business, the cost may be one of acquisition, in which case the amount of money expended to acquire it is counted as cost.

Cost engineering is the area of engineering practice where engineering judgment and experience are used in the application of scientific principles and techniques to problems of cost estimating, cost control, business planning and management science, profitability analysis, project management, and planning and scheduling."[

Construction, in the fields of architecture and civil engineering, is a process that consists of the building or assembling of infrastructure. Far from being a single activity, large scale construction is a feat of multitasking. Normally the job is managed by the project manager and supervised by the construction manager, design engineer, construction engineer or project architect.

Cost overrun is defined as excess of actual cost over budget.

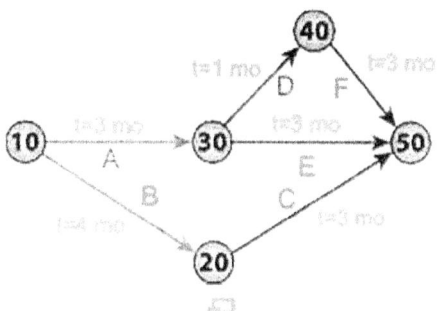

PERT chart with two critical paths.

Critical path method (CPM) is a mathematically based modeling technique for scheduling a set of project activities, used in project management.

Critical chain project management (CCPM) is a method of planning and managing projects that puts more emphasis on the resources required to execute project tasks.

D

Dependency in a project network is a link amongst a project's terminal elements.

Dynamic Systems Development Method (DSDM) is a software development methodology originally based upon the Rapid Application Development methodology. DSDM is an iterative and incremental approach that emphasizes continuous user involvement.

Duration of a project's terminal element is the number of calendar periods it takes from the time the execution of element starts to the moment it is completed.

Deliverable A contractually required work product, produced and delivered to a required state. A deliverable may be a document, hardware, software or other tangible product.

E

Earned schedule (ES) is an extension to earned value management (EVM), which renames two traditional measures, to indicate clearly they are in units of currency or quantity, not time.

Earned value management (EVM) is a project management technique for measuring project progress in an objective manner, with a combination of measuring scope, schedule, and cost in a single integrated system.

Effort management is a project management subdiscipline for effective and efficient use of time and resources to perform activities regarding quantity, quality and direction.

Enterprise modeling is the process of understanding an enterprise business and improving its performance through creation of enterprise models. This includes the modelling of the relevant business domain (usually relatively stable), business processes (usually more volatile), and Information technology

Estimation in project management is the processes of making accurate estimates using the appropriate techniques.

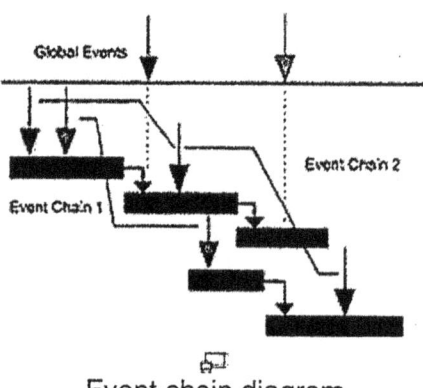
Event chain diagram

Event chain diagram : diagram that show the relationships between events and tasks and how the events affect each other.

Event chain methodology is an uncertainty modeling and schedule network analysis technique that is focused on identifying and managing events and event chains that affect project schedules.

Extreme project management (XPM) refers to a method of managing very complex and very uncertain projects.

F

Float in a project network is the amount of time that a task in a project network can be delayed without causing a delay to subsequent tasks and or the project completion date.

Focused Improvement in Theory of Constraints is the ensemble of activities aimed at elevating the performance of any system, especially a business system, with respect to its goal by eliminating its constraints one by one and by not working on non-constraints.

Fordism, named after Henry Ford, refers to various social theories. It has varying but related meanings in different fields, and for Marxist and non-Marxist scholars.

G

Henry Gantt was an American mechanical engineer and management consultant, who developed the Gantt chart in the 1910s.

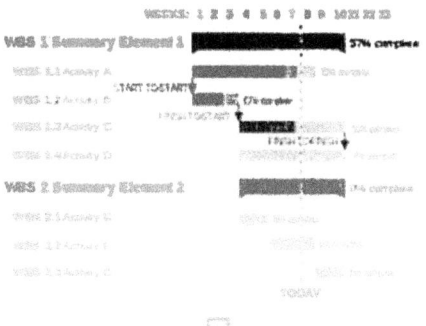

A Gantt chart.

Gantt chart is a type of bar chart that illustrates a project schedule. It illustrate the start and finish dates of the terminal elements and summary elements of a project. Terminal elements and summary elements comprise the work breakdown structure of the project.

Goal or objective consists of a projected state of affairs which a person or a system plans or intends to achieve or bring about — a personal or organizational desired end-point in some sort of assumed development. Many people endeavor to reach goals within a finite time by setting deadlines

Goal setting involves establishing specific, measurable and time targeted objectives

Graphical Evaluation and Review Technique (GERT) is a network analysis technique that allows probabilistic treatment of both network logic and activity duration estimated.

H

Hammock activity is a grouping of subtasks that "hangs" between two end dates it is tied to (or the two end-events it is fixed to).

HERMES is a Project Management Method developed by the Swiss Government, based on the German V-Modell. The first domain of application was software projects.

I

Integrated Master Plan (IMP) is an event-based, top level plan, consisting of a hierarchy of Program Events.

ISO 10006 is a guidelines for quality management in projects, is an international standard developed by the International Organization for Standardization.

Iterative and Incremental development is a cyclic software development process developed in response to the weaknesses of the waterfall model. It starts with an initial planning and ends with deployment with the cyclic interaction in between

K

Kickoff meeting is the first meeting with the project team and the client of the project.

L

Level of Effort (LOE) is qualified as a support type activity which doesn't lend itself to measurement of a discrete accomplishment. Examples of such an activity may be project budget accounting, customer liaison, etc.

Linear scheduling method (LSM) is a graphical scheduling method focusing on continuous resource utilization in repetitive activities. It is believed that it originally adopted the idea of Line-Of-Balance method.

Lean manufacturing or lean production, which is often known simply as "Lean", is the practice of a theory of production that considers the expenditure of resources for any means other than the creation of value for the presumed customer to be wasteful, and thus a target for elimination.

M

Management in business and human organization activity is simply the act of getting people together to accomplish desired goals. Management comprises planning, organizing, staffing, leading or directing, and controlling an organization (a group of one or more people or entities) or effort for the purpose of accomplishing a goal.

Management process is a process of planning and controlling the performance or execution of any type of activity.

Management science (MS), is the discipline of using mathematical modeling and other analytical methods, to help make better business management decisions.

Megaproject is an extremely large-scale investment project.

Motivation is the set of reasons that prompts one to engage in a particular behavior.

N

Nonlinear Management (NLM) is a superset of management techniques and strategies that allows order to emerge by giving organizations the space to self-organize, evolve and adapt, encompassing Agile, Evolutionary and Lean approaches, as well as many others.

O

Operations management is an area of business that is concerned with the production of good quality goods and services, and involves the responsibility of ensuring that business operations are efficient and effective. It is the management of resources, the distribution of goods and services to customers, and the analysis of queue systems.

Operations, see **Business operations**

Operations Research (OR) is an interdisciplinary branch of applied mathematics and formal science that uses methods such as mathematical modeling, statistics, and algorithms to arrive at optimal or near optimal solutions to complex problems.

Organization is a social arrangement which pursues collective goals, which controls its own performance, and which has a boundary separating it from its environment.

Organization development (OD) is a planned, structured, organization-wide effort to increase the organization's effectiveness and health.

P

Planning in organizations and public policy is both the organizational process of creating and maintaining a plan; and the psychological process of thinking about the activities required to create a desired goal on some scale.

Portfolio in finance is an appropriate mix of or collection of investments held by an institution or a private individual.

PRINCE2 : PRINCE2 is a project management methodology. The planning, monitoring and control of all aspects of the project and the motivation of all those involved in it to achieve the project objectives on time and to the specified cost, quality and performance.

Process is an ongoing collection of activities, with an inputs, outputs and the energy required to transform inputs to outputs.

Process architecture is the structural design of general process systems and applies to fields such as computers (software, hardware, networks, etc.), business processes (enterprise architecture, policy and procedures, logistics, project management, etc.), and any other process system of varying degrees of complexity.

Process management is the ensemble of activities of planning and monitoring the performance of a process, especially in the sense of business process, often confused with reengineering.

Product breakdown structure (PBS) in project management is an exhaustive, hierarchical tree structure of components that make up an item, arranged in whole-part relationship.

Product description in project management is a structured format of presenting information about a project product

Program Evaluation and Review Technique (PERT) is a statistical tool, used in project management, designed to analyze and represent the tasks involved in completing a given project.

Program Management is the process of managing multiple ongoing inter-dependent projects. An example would be that of designing, manufacturing and providing support infrastructure for an automobile manufacturer.

Project : A temporary endeavor undertaken to create a unique product, service, or result.

Project accounting Is the practice of creating financial reports specifically designed to track the financial progress of projects, which can then be used by managers to aid project management.

Project Cost Management A method of managing a project in real-time from the estimating stage to project control; through the use of technology cost, schedule and productivity is monitored.

Project management : The complete set of tasks, techniques, tools applied during project execution'.

Project Management Body of Knowledge (PMBOK) : The sum of knowledge within the profession of project management that is standardized by ISO.

Project management office: The Project management office in a business or professional enterprise is the department or group that defines and maintains the standards of process, generally related to project management, within the organization. The PMO strives to standardize and introduce economies of repetition in the execution of projects. The PMO is the source of documentation, guidance and metrics on the practice of project management and execution.

Project management process is the management process of planning and controlling the performance or execution of a project.

Project Management Professional is a certificated professional in project management.

Project Management Simulators are computer-based tools used in project management training programs. Usually, project management simulation is a group exercise. The computer-based simulation is an interactive learning activity.

Project management software is a type of software, including scheduling, cost control and budget management, resource allocation, collaboration software, communication, quality management and documentation or administration systems, which are used to deal with the complexity of large projects.

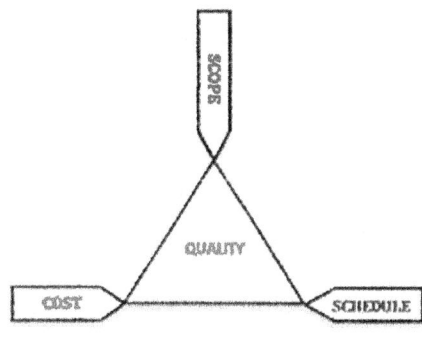

Project Management Triangle

Project Management Triangle is a model of the constraints of project management.

Project manager : professional in the field of project management. Project managers can have the responsibility of the planning, execution, and closing of any project, typically relating to construction industry, architecture, computer networking, telecommunications or software development.

Project network is a graph (flow chart) depicting the sequence in which a project's terminal elements are to be completed by showing terminal elements and their dependencies.

Project plan is a formal, approved document used to guide both *project execution* and *project control*. The primary uses of the project plan are to document planning assumptions and decisions, facilitate communication among *stakeholders*, and document approved scope, cost, and schedule *baselines*. A project plan may be summary or detailed.

Project planning is part of project management, which relates to the use of schedules such as Gantt charts to plan and subsequently report progress within the project environment.

Project stakeholders are those entities within or without an organization which sponsor a project or, have an interest or a gain upon a successful completion of a project.

Project team is the management team leading the project, and provide services to the project. Projects often bring together a variety number of problems. Stakeholders have important issues with others.

Proport refers to the combination of the unique skills of an organisation's members for collective advantage.

Q

Quality can mean a high degree of excellence ("a quality product"), a degree of excellence or the lack of it ("work of average quality"), or a property of something ("the addictive quality of alcohol").[1] Distinct from the vernacular, the subject of this article is the business interpretation of quality.

Quality, Cost, Delivery(QCD) as used in lean manufacturing measures a businesses activity and develops Key performance indicators. QCD analysis often forms a part of continuous improvement programs

R

Reengineering is radical redesign of an organization's processes, especially its business processes. Rather than organizing a firm into functional specialties (like production, accounting, marketing, etc.) and considering the tasks that each function performs; complete processes from materials acquisition, to production, to marketing and distribution should be considered. The firm should be re-engineered into a series of processes.

Resources are what is required to carry out a project's tasks. They can be people, equipment, facilities, funding, or anything else capable of definition (usually other than labour) required for the completion of a project activity.

Risk is the precise probability of specific eventualities.

Risk management is a management specialism aiming to reduce different risks related to a preselected domain to the level accepted by society. It may refer to numerous types of threats caused by environment, technology, humans, organizations and politics.

Risk register is a tool commonly used in project planning and organizational risk assessments.

S

Schedules in project management consists of a list of a project's terminal elements with intended start and finish dates.

Scientific management is a theory of management that analyzes and synthesizes workflow processes, improving labor productivity.

Scope of a project in project management is the sum total of all of its products and their requirements or features.

Scope creep refers to uncontrolled changes in a project's scope. This phenomenon can occur when the scope of a project is not properly defined, documented, or controlled. It is generally considered a negative occurrence that is to be avoided.

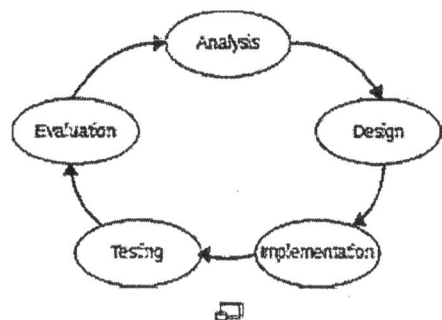

The systems development life cycle.

Scrum is an iterative incremental process of software development commonly used with agile software development. Despite the fact that "Scrum" is not an acronym, some companies implementing the process have been known to adhere to an all capital letter expression of the word, i.e. SCRUM.

Six Sigma is a business management strategy, originally developed by Motorola, that today enjoys widespread application in many sectors of industry.

Software engineering is the application of a systematic, disciplined, quantifiable approach to the development, operation, and maintenance of software.[1]

Systems Development Life Cycle (SDLC) is any logical process used by a systems analyst to develop an information system, including requirements, validation, training, and user ownership. An SDLC should result in a high quality system that meets or exceeds customer expectations, within time and cost estimates, works effectively and efficiently in the current and planned Information Technology infrastructure, and is cheap to maintain and cost-effective to enhance.

Systems engineering is an interdisciplinary field of engineering that focuses on how complex engineering projects should be designed and managed.

T

Task is part of a set of actions which accomplish a job, problem or assignment.

Tasks in project management are activity that needs to be accomplished within a defined period of time.

Task analysis is the analysis or a breakdown of exactly how a task is accomplished, such as what sub-tasks are required

Timeline is a graphical representation of a chronological sequence of events, also referred to as a chronology. It can also mean a schedule of activities, such as a timetable.

U

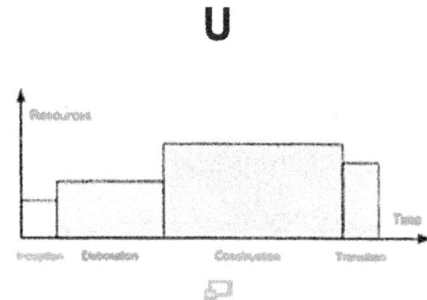

The Unified Process.

Unified Process: The Unified process is a popular iterative and incremental software development process framework. The best-known and extensively documented refinement of the Unified Process is the Rational Unified Process (RUP).

V

Value engineering (VE) is a systematic method to improve the "value" of goods and services by using an examination of function. Value, as defined, is the ratio of function to cost. Value can therefore be increased by either improving the function or reducing the cost. It is a primary tenet of value engineering that basic functions be preserved and not be reduced as a consequence of pursuing value improvements.

Vertical slice is a type of milestone, benchmark, or deadline, with emphasis on demonstrating progress across all components of a project.

Virtual Design and Construction (VDC) is the use of integrated multi-disciplinary performance models of design-construction projects, including the Product (i.e., facilities), Work Processes and Organization of the design - construction - operation team in order to support explicit and public business objectives.

W

Wideband Delphi is a consensus-based estimation technique for estimating effort.

Work in project management is the amount of effort applied to produce a deliverable or to accomplish a task (a terminal element).

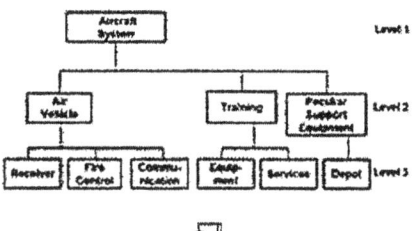
A work breakdown structure.

Work Breakdown Structure (WBS) is a tool that defines a project and groups the project's discrete work elements in a way that helps organize and define the total work scope of the project. A Work breakdown structure element may be a product, data, a service, or any combination. WBS also provides the necessary framework for detailed cost estimating and control along with providing guidance for schedule development and control.

Work package is a subset of a project that can be assigned to a specific party for execution. Because of the similarity, work packages are often misidentified as projects.

Workstream is a set of associated activities, focused around a particular scope that follow a path from initiation to completion.